BRANSON'S ENTERTAINMENT PIONEERS

About this book

In 1960 in the small, riverfront Ozark town, Branson, Missouri the beginnings of one of the most unusual towns in America were just barely discernible. Those involved in the endeavor were simply trying to make a living—paying their bills and supporting their families. They had absolutely no idea of the magnitude to which their early efforts would grow.

This is the story of those first Branson entertainers as they traveled an uncharted course—in a most unlikely place. In 1960 a few thousand visitors vacationed in Branson. Fifty years later, in 2010, an estimated eight million visitors will visit the town. It's a success story with few equals and the achievement rests on the efforts of these first entertainment pioneers.

About the author

Robert McGill, a native Ozarker, has been an active observer of the Branson entertainment scene much his life. As a child he remembers family Sunday outings to view the construction of Table Rock Dam, the early days of Silver Dollar City, and attending the very first music shows in Branson.

During a period during the late 1970's and early 1980's he rarely missed seeing every music show with his family.

He has written extensively about the Ozarks.

McGill holds both a bachelors and masters degree from the University of Missouri, Columbia and a Ph. D. from the Union Institute and University, Cincinnati, Ohio.

BRANSON'S ENTERTAINMENT PIONEERS

by Robert McGill

Acknowledgements

One of the joys of my childhood growing up in the Ozarks was to visit Branson and Silver Dollar City on family outings. These visits spurred my lifelong fascination with the area.

Later, in the mid 1970's, I was employed at Galena, Missouri, a distance of forty miles from Branson. At that time, with a family of my own, we attempted to attend every show in Branson as well as Silver Dollar City—the Shepherd of the Hills Outdoor Drama, the Baldknobbers, the Presleys' Country Jubilee, the Foggy River Boys, the Bob-O-Link's, and on and on it went, for several years. We watched the town develop and often heard the skeptical question so common throughout the Ozarks "Branson's doing fine, but it sure won't last, will it?"

I wrote my first article about Branson in the late 1980's for a book that I published, *In the Heart of Ozark Mountain Country,* and for that article conducted my first interview with several people who are a part of this book, Peter Herschend, Peter Engler, Bill, Bob, and Lyle Mabe, Lloyd and Bessie Mae Presley, and Bob Hubbard. All told stories about their participation in the development of Branson.

Twenty years later, in the early 2000's, I was the director of Ozark Adventures, a not-for-profit organization in Branson, which decided to archive the stories of the men and families who created the entertainment industry. Thus, I was able, again, to interview many of the same people that I had interviewed twenty years earlier—Bob Mabe, Randy Plummer and, in a second separate interview, Randy, Darrell and Rosie Plummer, Peter Engler, Jack Herschend, Lloyd, Steve, and Gary Presley, Bob Dixon, and Bob Hubbard. Sarah Klinefelter took the lead in interviewing Mark Trimble. Dick Erickson conducted the second interview with the Plummer family and was a tremendous help throughout the whole process of conducting these interviews. In follow up conversations, at least one member of each of the venues has generously given time and encouragement to this project.

In particular, I want to acknowledge the story Kathy Van Buskirk wrote on the Shepherd of the Hills for the book, *In the Heart of Ozark Mountain Country*. Kathy was a very careful historian and good storyteller.

Many have contributed to the content of this book. In particular, I want to thank a former officemate, Karen Pugh, for her several suggestions and Beverly and Keith O'Neil and Cyndi Strecky for their insights into Branson. The newspaper articles and book, *Branson, the Music Show Capitol of the World,* by Jimmy Lancaster, the tenacious entertainment reporter for the Branson Daily News during the 1990's, were also most helpful. Dan Lennon of the Branson Chamber of Commerce has provided information, as did Tom Deboe. Mark Trimble, Evelyn Fullerton, Keith Thurman, and Jean Babcock have supplied photographs as well as Martha Hoy Bohner and Lisa Rau from Silver Dollar City.

My heartfelt thanks to all who have made a contribution.

A special thank you also goes to my three children, Heather, Chris, and Denise for the wonderful memories from their childhood when together we attended Silver Dollar City and the Branson music shows. Denise has supplied the fiddle photograph on page 28.

Thank you, Karlene, for your love and support throughout the research and writing of this book.

Diana Ross has taken on and ably fulfilled the often arduous task as editor of this book.

Dixie Blevins has completed the preparation of this manuscript for printing.

Book cover and graphic design by Beverly O'Neil.

BRANSON'S ENTERTAINMENT PIONEERS

by Robert McGill

White Oak Publishing
P.O. Box 188
Reeds Spring, MO 65737

ISBN 978-0-935069-11-2

First Edition

BRANSON'S ENTERTAINMENT PIONEERS

Table of Contents

During placid times the White River, and its tributary, the James River, provided world-renowned float fishing. Prior to 1960, catering to fishermen was Branson's major industry.

Raging floods on the White River, like this one in 1928 inundated downtown Branson and eventually lead to the construction of Table Rock Dam.

Branson 1960

In the spring of 1960, many Branson residents felt a lingering apprehension. Just two summers before, seven miles west of town, the massive gates of a new dam on the White River which flowed through Branson, had been closed. Dedication ceremonies had been held the previous year, on June 14. The dam, created to form Table Rock Lake, inundated one of the most magnificent river valleys in North America.

The building of the dam had been championed for years, notably by Republican Congressman Dewey Short, a staunch conservative from nearby Galena, Missouri. Short cited the need for both flood control and the generation of electricity, advocating the building of the dam as early as 1929. As a boy, the Congressman actually made his spending money by delivering ice to fishermen on the James River arm of the White River, as they prepared to float-fish the rivers. As a Congressman, who later became an arch opponent of the depression-era policies of President Roosevelt, he believed in the necessity of the dam and felt the authorization of funds from Congress would be forthcoming.

It was not, however, until the early 1950's, after the Great Depression of the 1930's and World War II, that a Branson banker, Democrat Ben Parnell, took up the task of lobbying Congress for funds. Banker Parnell believed that Branson, with a population of only 1875 residents, had languished for years, seeing its few young people, upon graduating from high school, immediately leave the area for more education, employment, and career opportunities. For them, remaining in Branson was economic suicide. Few ever returned except to visit the families left behind. To remedy this, Parnell and other businessmen believed the dam construction would allow the Branson area to prosper. Parnell lobbied for the building of the dam, particularly with influential Missouri U.S. Senator Stuart Symington. As Secretary of the Army from 1947 to 1950, Stuart Symington became acquainted with five-star general Dwight Eisenhower, a popular World War II hero who had commanded the allied landing on Normandy. When Eisenhower became President in a landslide victory in 1952, Symington was able to persuade him to include the costs of the dam in his 1954 budget to Congress. The building of the dam began the following year, to be completed in 1958.

The closing of the gates effectively stopped the town's major industry, catering to float fishermen on the beautiful White River. The lives of many of the townspeople and river men were forever changed. Gone, too, were many of the farmers who tilled the small farms of the White River valley. Their farms now lay under hundreds of feet of water. Only the few lakeside cabins and restaurants remained, catering to the handful of tourists who wanted only a few days of peace and quiet to roam

The construction of Table Rock Dam, completed in 1958 with dedication ceremonies in 1959, spurred the development of the tourist industry in Branson.

Passenger rail service to Bramsom was discontinued in 1960, assuring that the town would be built on automobile and coach trafffic. The year marked the beginning of the current tourist industry.

the countryside and relax. A few of these tourists made their way out to the Shepherd of the Hills Homestead or to Marvel Cave, but they were not big spenders, nor were there many of them. To grow, Branson would need an economic infusion. Perhaps, because of the new lake, it could grow from its fledging tourism base.

Already a young, enterprising resident named Mark Trimble was wandering around town, recruiting local residents to perform in a rather audacious venture he was planning. He wanted to create an outdoor drama based on the nationally famous book, *The Shepherd of the Hills.* The book had been written by author Harold Bell Wright fifty years earlier, with much of the story taking place just west of Branson on Dewey Bald Mountain. Since Branson was the setting for the book, its publication had brought renown to the area. Mark's parents owned the property where Harold Bell Wright had camped during his stay, and Mark believed an outdoor drama might draw visitors to Branson and the family farm, the Shepherd of the Hills Homestead.

Marvel Cave also existed in 1960, offering another possibility for drawing more visitors to the area. Mary Herschend, along with her two young sons, Jack and Peter, already operated a thriving business guiding tourists through the cave. Only the year before, they had held a press conference announcing the building of a small craft town, Silver Dollar City, next to the cave entrance. The Herschends invited a Hillbilly band from nearby Nixa to provide entertainment at the press conference. Townspeople knew that Mary Herschend had a strong character and that her two sons were industrious. Maybe, they thought, building a new tourist village would attract some tourists. Although skeptical, they hoped for the best.

Nationally, there was reason to believe that tourism might take hold in Branson. In 1960, the nation was experiencing a period of

This road, at one time Highway 80, made its way along the east side of Joe Bald Mountain before curving back in front of the Shepherd of the Hills Homestead on its way west. Vastly improved, the road is now Highway 76 and passes not only The Shepherd of the Hills Outdoor Drama but also Silver Dollar City.

unprecedented optimism and prosperity. Finally, after the recession of the 30's and the war of the 40's, the economy had recovered sufficiently to build an affluent America. Wages were rising. Nice new suburban housing developments were extending for miles outside major cities. The new interstate transportation system was reaching completion. High speed highways ribboned out across the country, allowing car owners to travel almost any place in the nation they cared to go. The average wage was nearly $5,000 a year, a sufficient amount to feed, clothe, and house a family, with a little pocket change left over at the end of the month. In 1960 American families had spending money, an automobile, and a road system—the prerequisites for an American vacation.

In embracing this affluent new future, it is interesting to note that Branson offered an entertainment that was firmly anchored in the past. These first two attractions, the outdoor drama at the Shepherd of the Hills and the 1880's themed village, Silver Dollar City, while vastly different, were both based on a small slice of Ozark history and culture. Both became immensely successful.

As the entertainment pioneers in Branson would discover, there was a huge niche in the vacationing market of American travelers who, rather than searching out the biggest, best, and most audacious new entertainment of an affluent era, were instead attracted to what they knew–the safe and the familiar. Themes of the past attracted their attention. It was as if a segment of vacationing Americans understood that while the vast American scene was undergoing significant change, to be propelled into the future they must first be grounded in the past. From the beginning, Branson's venues struck a national chord, and in so doing and in the due course of time, turned Branson into one of the most unusual towns in America.

Locally renowned, pipe smoking taxi driver Pearl Spurlock, standing next to her 1939 Buick Taxi Cab.

Above: Joe Bald Mountain on the north edge of Branson. Much of the story in The Shepherd of the Hills took place on this mountain.

Left: J.K and Anna Ross, models for the fictional characters Old Matt and Aunt Mollie.

For five summers, beginning in 1955, college students from Southern Illinois University and Central Missouri State College, joined local residents in a drama workshop on the Branson riverfront. On Saturday nights, the players presented The Shepherd of the Hills.

The Shepherd of the Hills

An amazing act of kindness at the turn of the 20th century lead to the current Branson entertainment scene. In 1901, J. K. and Anna Ross extended an offer of help to a young stranger who appeared at their farm, an aspiring author, Harold Bell Wright, near Dewey Bald Mountain, just five miles west of downtown Branson. J. K. and Anna lived in a small log cabin and occasionally befriended and boarded strangers who appeared in the area. Wright's first visit to the Ozarks occurred the previous year, in 1900 when Wright, fearful he had contracted tuberculosis, decided to go to Springfield, Missouri, to visit his uncle and rest. The two descended into the mountains south of Springfield for an outing, going into the White Oak District, an area that included the current town of Branson. The short stay introduced Wright to the scenic beauty of the Ozarks. Even in that brief period he fell in love with the hills and valleys and the people he met. He quickly came to believe the people of the region mirrored what he believed to be exemplary lifestyles.

The charm of the Ozarks lured him to return on horseback the following year to the Ross homestead, where he pitched his tent in anticipation of writing his notes for his second book, *The Shepherd of the Hills*. He spent the summer roaming the countryside and exploring even further into the life of the mountain folks, intent on learning more about their habits and customs, hopes and dreams. When he left at summer's end, Wright took a rough draft of his book with him.

Wright was young, in his mid- twenties at the time he wrote the book. Born in Rome, New York, he had lived a nomadic life. His only close boyhood companion, his mother, died when he was ten years old at which time the precocious young man came under the care of his father. However, his father, a civil war veteran, could never settle down. He moved constantly as he plied his trade as an itinerant carpenter and house painter while frequenting back-alley saloons and houses of bawdy conduct. Usually, during these moves, he kept Harold at his side, although at times he sent the young boy to live with relatives. At first, Wright retained his father's trade as a house painter, but rejected his way of life. In a reversal of that lifestyle, Wright became a minister and teacher of moral principals. Later, his books would embody these themes of his personal beliefs.

Undoubtedly, on this second extended stay, Wright became even more enchanted with the Ozarks. For not only did he find an abundance of material for this second book, which became hugely successful, but the area also became the setting for many of his later novels. The popularity of *The Shepherd of the Hills* helped focus a continuing stream of

Author Harold Bell Wright

attention on the Branson area. The impact was still obvious in 1960, when the current scene of Branson tourism began.

Wright modeled several of his fictional characters on the individuals living in the Branson vicinity. The story chronicled the time of quiet upheaval that he found in the agrarian Ozarks. He wove together several themes, combining the unsettling stories of the Civil War and the local vigilante group, the Baldknobbers, which formed in its aftermath. Since both the first roads for automobiles and railroad tracks were being constructed into the valley below the Ross homestead, he wrote of the formidable impact he believed both would have on the lives of the people in the community. To heighten the drama, he added the drought that plagued the countryside during his stay. The area, he believed, would cease to remain an isolated backwoods locale, once civilization came ever nearer.

Local author Kathy Van Buskirk characterized the story in this way:

> *The Shepherd of the Hills is fiction, an imagined tale woven around the hilltop cabin and the people Wright found living there. He models Old Matt, Aunt Mollie, and Young Matt on the Rosses {a local family}, adding a daughter to the fictional Matthews family. Into the Matthews' lives comes a gentle, religious stranger from the city, who tends sheep and soon becomes "shepherd" to his neighbors as well. No one knows that the shepherd's son and the Matthews' daughter have, in past years, been secret lovers. After her lover has left the area, the girl dies giving birth to a son, the strange child known as "Little Pete." Grief-stricken Old Matt bitterly hates the man he believes caused his daughter's death.*

The novel is a story of betrayal, guilt, love, and, ultimately, redemption. The book struck a chord with readers across the nation and became a national best-seller. Within a few years, it sold 17 million copies, making it at one time the fourth largest selling book in U. S. history.

Jacket of a video showing John Wayne as Young Matt.

Upon publication, visitors began trekking into the Branson area to visit the rustic Shepherd of the Hills homestead of J. K and Anna Ross and to meet the people upon whom the book was based. Many visitors failed to realize the book was fiction and locals often conveniently failed to tell them otherwise. Residents were covetous of the fact that a popular book had been written in and about the area.

No less than five different movies were made of the book. The first two were silent movies filmed immediately after the release of the book, the first produced by the author himself. Production for the second picture, filmed a decade later, was begun in Branson. However, producers cited rising production costs and took actors, cameras, and other production equipment back to Hollywood to complete the shooting of the picture. No existing copies of this film exist today. Stars for the third film, released in 1941, included two well-known actors of the day, Harry Cary and Betty Field, while the starring role of young Matt went to a new but "up-and-coming" actor named John Wayne. Unfortunately, this adaptation of the book resembled the original work in only the slightest of

Dr. Bruce Trimble

Mrs. Mary Trimble

Even in his youth, Mark Trimble was an avid pilot

ways—the film story was about a young hillbilly moonshiner intent on seeking family revenge for indignities his family had suffered—and the film was shot in the Pine country of California rather than within the Oak forests of the Ozarks. Reportedly, incensed Wright family members received apologies from the producers for the lax treatment of the book. Nevertheless, the release of each film version of the book spurred an additional stream of visitors into Branson to visit the setting of the book. Still another version was filmed in Branson in 1959 by local Springfield television station KY3 and featured local actors Hal Meadows, Shad Heller, and several others who starred in the outdoor drama. While a very faithful adaptation of the book, this version was never released for national syndication. The final filming, in 1964, included both Hollywood and local actors. This version starred Richard Arlen as Old Matt and James Bradford as the Sheriff, but included local actors Shad Heller, James Collie, and Lloyd Durre.

The impact of the best selling book was so great that during the 1930's and beyond Missouri tourism officials marketed all of southwest Missouri as Shepherd of the Hills Country. For nearly half a century, tourist oriented brochures and maps beckoning visitors into the region would feature the beauty and scenery of the mountains, the valley streams, and the welcoming nature of the residents, calling it all Shepherd of the Hills Country. The book and its legacy fared well.

But, the Ross homestead did not do so well. When the Ross's died, the property fell into disrepair until Lizzie McDaniel, a Springfield resident, purchased the property in 1926. Her hopes were to restore the cabin, homestead, and mill to their original condition. Her efforts helped maintain and partially restore the sadly neglected property. Lizzie opened the homestead to visitors, produced a small pageant based on the novel, and collected memorabilia for the cabin.

By 1945 the property had again fallen into disrepair, having passed through the ownership of several people. This time the property was purchased by a retired professor and his wife, Dr. Bruce and Mrs. Mary Trimble, from Kansas City, who were eager to preserve the historical significance of the farmstead. They devoted their own money and effort into rebuilding the farmstead and constructing an outdoor amphitheater. The Trimbles purchased the 160 acre property for $12,000 dollars, a huge sum at the time since much of the rough Ozark land could be purchased for $5.00 an acre.

Dr. Trimble died in 1957 leaving his wife Mary and young son Mark to continue the family business. Mark, a graduate of Branson High School, was attending the University of Arkansas in Fayetteville, daily flying his own Culver 5 airplane

Opening night at the Shepherd of the Hills Outdoor Drama, August 5, 1960.

to classes. This cut the 112 mile distance, often over rutted Ozark roads, nearly in half.

In 1960, having only recently returned from military service, Mark was intent on closing the family business and selling the Shepherd of the Hills farmstead. But the possibilities of launching a successful entrepreneurial enterprise enhanced by the building of the new dam pricked his interest. Perhaps, he decided, conditions were ripe for success. After several conversations with his mother, Mark decided that if the historical farmstead were to be restored and an amphitheater built, it would be up to the two to do so. They set to work to produce the play, the effort challenging the abilities of both the young man and his mother, who was soon struck with a debilitating illness.

Mark joined with local actor Shad Heller, (we'll hear more about him later) James Colley, a professor and playwright from a small college in Coffeyville, Kansas, and Dixon Baker, an advertising executive from Springfield, to coordinate the development of the play, making it suitable for a performance in an outdoor amphitheater. Local workmen built a small, adequate amphitheater on the hillside of the Homestead. The building for the old gristmill, the same one that was in use when Wright visited the property, was still intact, although badly in need of repair. Mark found an old Case steam engine, identical to the original engine, and when another local resident gave him a pair of burrs for the mill, the restoration was complete. Two-hundred seventy-five canvas backed chairs served as seats for audience members. Mark himself scouted the local area for acting talent—many of the townspeople were cast to suitable parts—a few weeks of nightly practice and the first performance was presented August 5, 1960. The crew and cast accomplished their mission that first year, continuing performances throughout the fall fishing season.

The outdoor drama was not a professional production, nor was it amateurish, even though featuring local residents who were often responsible for adapting the script, developing their own characters, acting, and producing their own play. The pride and satisfaction of the actors and producers, and, indeed, the power of the authenticity of the production became self evident. Audience members were made well aware from advanced advertising that the drama was performed by local residents, and they identified with the pride local participants evoked at their own efforts. On

A vigilante group, the Baldknobbers, whose members wore hoods, existed in the area in the 1880's.

opening night, Mark, playing the part of a stranger, spoke the very first words explaining to audience members that the scenes depicted in the play were the same scenes described by the author Wright as having taken place on that very same site. Audience members were seeing an authentic reproduction of the play.

Yet, in their efforts to be faithful to the story, locals knew the authenticity might have even gone to extreme. During a stretch of time during one of the early seasons, the characters cast as tough outlaws who were required to be chased, riding horseback across the outdoor stage, could not be present for the performance. Finding last-minute replacements skilled in riding horses took some ingenuity, but young Mark knew that his friend, the county sheriff, had some local rascals locked up in his country jail who could ride horseback. Through this connection, Mark was able to secure the release of the men for a few days, until his permanent cast members returned—at which time the real ruffians were sent back to jail.

These early cast members were also responsible for all aspects of the production, selling tickets, ushering in guests, operating the light and sound consoles, and cleaning up the amphitheater after every performance. One cast member, Neil Klinefelter, relates that the crew had help with clean-up every night, for they knew a den of skunks lurked in the woods just outside the sight of guests. Inevitably, at every performance, guests would spill kernels of popcorn and candy crumbs in the aisles of the arena. The skunks conditioned themselves to know when the play ended, then would amble out of the nearby woods as the audience exited. The clean-up crew always allowed the skunks to pass through the aisles first, cleaning up the morsels before walking down and sweeping the aisles with their own brooms. During those early days, more than one exiting guest panicked upon seeing a skunk following them down the aisle, picking up their spilled food as they left the theater.

The production was tremendously successful. Customers at first trickled in, then began arriving in ever increasing numbers as enthusiastic audience members applauded the performance. Within a few short years the outdoor drama became the largest outdoor production in the United States, at a time when other outdoor productions also were flourishing. The restored homestead and greatly expanded amphitheater became a "must see" attraction for visitors to Branson.

One particular set of performers, the four versatile Mabe Brothers, performed not only in several different parts of the drama, but were also involved in other entertainment efforts in the area. These were the same Mabe Brothers who had begun calling themselves the Baldknobbers only the year before, when the Herschends invited them to play at the press conference announcing the opening of Silver Dollar City. In The Shepherd of the Hills drama

Cast members square dance during a performance.

An early and popular publicity photograph of Sammy Lane, Young Matt, and the Old Shepherd at Old Matts Cabin.

one of the brothers, Bob, served as the sheriff, bringing law and order to the respectable citizens of the countryside. As a posse, the brothers galloped their horses across the arena in pursuit of the bad outlaws who menaced the upright citizens of the fictional community each night. And, at intermission, the brothers became a country music band and invited guests down to the old mill to square dance while they provided the live music. The Baldknobbers continued in the Shepherd of the Hills production for two years. In addition, that first year they also began performing on weekends on a regular basis in the downtown community building, establishing themselves as Branson's first musical show.

The success of the outdoor drama hinged on advertising. Mark Trimble recognized early on that visitors came to Branson because it was, in marketing parlance, a destination—and once in Branson, tourists would visit more than one attraction. Thus, he reasoned, his marketing dollars should promote not only his own production, but the area as a whole. And the same was true of other venues in Branson. There was much to see and do: the beauty of the Ozark Mountains, the recreation on the new lake, the other developing attraction, Silver Dollar City, the newly developing music shows downtown, and his own Shepherd of the Hills drama. Mark reasoned that more visitors would come and spend several days, or a whole vacation, if they knew all that was available.

To promote Branson as a destination, in 1971 Mark joined with Jack and Peter Herschend of Silver Dollar City, and Pat Jones, the father of current Dallas Cowboy owner, Jerry Jones, who owned a drive-through exotic animal paradise east of Springfield. Pat's attraction allowed visitors to view deer, elk, buffalo, and other large, wild animals from the safety of their cars—an opportunity many families found highly appealing. Together, they formed a joint marketing effort. With Peter Herschend as the president of the group, the three pooled part of their advertising dollars to pay for the inclusion of a descriptive flyer in the Sunday supplements of many of the larger newspapers in the Midwest. The theme became "Ozark Fun in 71." The success of the advertising campaign was extraordinary. Visitors to the area surged upwards, resulting in the formation of the Ozark Marketing Council, a group of local businesses who collectively advertised Branson, at first in print with newspapers, and then through prime time television commercials. The marketing council soon expanded so that even the smallest resort owners and restaurateurs could join with the largest attractions in extending their advertising efforts. The council played an important part in Branson's growth until it merged with the Branson Chamber of Commerce in the mid 1980's.

Civilization comes to the Ozarks.

A fight scene from the play.

However, Mark also had his own personal method of tallying visitors to Branson. In the later 1970's and '80's, as more theaters and attractions developed in Branson, Mark would rev up his own Culver V airplane and, as dusk approached, fly over the strip, counting the cars in the parking lots of the various venues. In this way he became quite proficient at keeping tabs on the number of visitors to Branson each night.

The mid 1980's was also the time when Mark Trimble sold the Shepherd of the Hills Homestead to local residents Gary and Pat Snadon, who continued developing the farmstead and producing the drama. Mark stayed in the tourist business for a few years, building a showroom for his collection of restored vintage automobiles before finally selling that building to another area businessman, Allen Johnson and his partner, as a theater. The new owners enticed a young Branson entertainer, Shoji Tabuchi, to become their first tenant. Shoji later became one of Branson's first superstars.

Mark Trimble had returned home from military service in the late 1950's with the intention of cleaning up the Shepherd of the Hills Homestead and selling the property. He still laughs at that notion. It took him thirty-five years to accomplish the task—and along the way he became one of Branson's first entertainment pioneers.

Silver Dollar City

On May 1, 1960, Silver Dollar City, an attraction that would immediately impact the Branson area and dominate the tourist trade for fifty years, opened its gates to visitors for the first time. Development came about following a vision of what might possibly develop and the perceptive decisions of one family, Hugo Herschend, his wife Mary, and their two sons, Jack and Peter. Their efforts began in 1949 when Hugo, the visionary of the family, signed a long term lease obtaining control of a picturesque hillside property west of Branson. The property contained Marvel Cave, a cave that featured many beautiful and unusual geological formations. The property bordered on what would become Highway 76, nine miles west of Branson. From that inauspicious beginning, their endeavors have developed into the largest family-owned entertainment corporation in America, Herschend Family Entertainment. Thus, the story of Silver Dollar begins with the history of a cave—a cave that is still an integral part of the City.

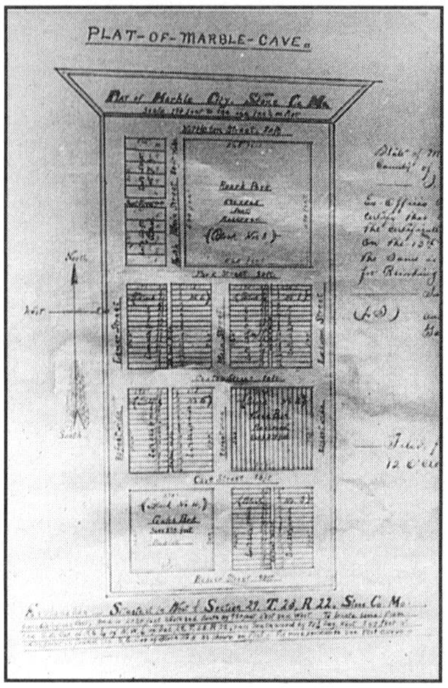

A copy of the plat of Marvel City filed in 1884 at the courthouse in Galena, Stone County, Mo.

The initial plat of the cave and hillside was filed in 1884 at the courthouse in Galena, Missouri, by veteran Civil War officers from Lamar, Missouri, who discovered the cave during one of their war forays. These veterans believed that one of the sheer walls inside the cave was actually marble and they knew that bat guano lay piled high on the cave floor. They hoped to mine the guano and eventually find a market for the marble. The plat mapped out a mining town and stage coach stop, named Marble City, at the mouth of the cave. Over the next several years, although the mining ceased and the property changed hands several times, a small, roughly built town actually developed. Even after the Herschends took control of the property in 1949, vestiges of a sawmill, livery stable, stage coach stop, pottery and furniture factory, and boarding house could be found on the hillside behind the cave.

In 1889 the original owners of the property found a purchaser, an unlikely buyer, Dr. William Lynch, a dairy farmer from Canada. Dr Lynch, along with his two daughters, Genevieve, a registered nurse and poet, and Marian, an opera singer and instructor, purchased the property for $10,000. They hoped even at that early date to open the cave for sightseers.

The Lynches began operation of their commercial venture in 1894 with a grand celebration and a few visitors. But at that time William Lynch was not able to make the cave profitable. He returned to Canada for several years to raise additional capital

The Lynch Sisters standing in front of Marvel Cave Lodge. They operated the cave business for almost 50 years.

before returning, sometime after 1900, with his daughters to reopen the cave. The cave has remained open since then, making it one of the oldest continuously running tourist attractions in the Ozarks. It was sometime during this period that it was discovered the sheer, glossy wall of the cave was not marble, but limestone, and so the cave was renamed Marvel Cave.

The Lynches operated the cave for nearly fifty years. At first, tourists arrived on horseback or in animal-drawn carriages by traveling the old trail running from Springfield through the nearby town of Reeds Spring to Marvel Cave.

Then, after building the railroad in the early 1900's through Roark Valley between Reeds Spring and Branson, visitors could request that the engineer stop the train at a small switch station, a rail stop named Gretna, below the cave. From that point, they made their way up the hill. When motorized vehicles arrived in the Ozarks, the trail from Springfield was the first motor route to Marvel Cave. Finally, in the 1930's, when the road to Branson was constructed over Dewey Bald Mountain past the Shepherd of the Hills Homestead, tourists could also arrive by vehicle from the east.

The early entrance into Marvel Cave.

The early expeditions into the cave were strenuous. Visitors were issued candles and tough, leather-seated coveralls. They climbed down a rickety ladder that dropped seventy-five feet through darkness to a steep hill inside the cave. Visitors could spend a full day exploring the passageways, crevices, and tunnels with a guide. They exited up the same ladder they had climbed down. Few other improvements marked the cave although a piano was lowered into the cave so that on special occasions Miss Miriam could give opera recitals.

When William Lynch died on September 13, 1927, at age 80, ownership of the cave passed to his two daughters, Miss Miriam and Miss Genevieve, who operated the cave for the next twenty-three years.

The Lynch sisters lived in a small lodge and frequently rented rooms to their guests. Although they personally cooked many of the guest meals and often served them outside on a long lawn table, they hired guides to lead tours through the cave. Several people who later became important to Silver Dollar City as guides, builders, and craftsmen were originally employed by the sisters as cave guides. One of the first was Ott Teague, at the time a newlywed living on Roark Creek, who carted visitors from the railroad switch in Roark Valley up the hill to the Lynch Lodge. When he saw tourists arriving, a skinny young boy named Lester Vining would catch the Lynch sisters' goats and tie them up so they would not disturb the cave visitors. From the nearby town of Reeds Spring, Fannabelle Nickel, a lover of pets and small animals, later became the mother-in-law of one of the new lessees, Jack Herschend. The Lynch's retained control of the cave and surrounding property until 1949 when Hugo negotiated the 99 year lease to the property.

Hugo Herschend - the family visionary. Mary Herschend - She brought Hugo's visions to fruition with the completion of improvments to Marvel Cave and the construction of Silver Dollar City. Peter & Jack Herschend - Through their combined efforts, Silver Dollar City developed into the largest family owned entertainment corporation in America.

The Herschend family first began visiting the area on vacations in the mid 1940's. Hugo, who had enjoyed a successful career as a vacuum cleaner salesman, was looking for a retirement project. He liked the peacefulness and serenity of the Ozarks and felt that the Branson area would be an excellent place to raise his sons, thus leading to the decision to settle in the Ozarks. The two boys were delighted since they had the only parents they knew in all of Chicago who operated a cave.

For Hugo, a visionary, the development of the property was a challenge. He quickly formed fascinating new ideas for improving the interior of the cave and developing cave tours. Indeed, his dreams for the property extended beyond the cave, to developing the property above ground. Eventually, he hoped, a small craft village would be constructed on the premises as a market outlet where local skilled and hardworking—but meagerly paid craftsmen—could sell their woodworking, carvings, and white oak baskets to area visitors. He wanted to develop the full potential of the property.

But Hugo knew that the implementation for his ideas would not come easily. For one thing, in order to raise needed capital, Hugo had to live in Chicago much of the time to tend to his Chicago business. This forced Mary and the two boys to travel to the Ozarks each summer to conduct tours of the cave and expand the operation, although she was a trained librarian with very little business experience.

In their first summer at the cave the new operators welcomed 8,000 visitors. For the next three years the Herschends hosted summer tourists and made modest improvements in the cave. It took four years for the Herchends to turn their first profit from the cave venture.

The Herschends first efforts were to improve the entrance and exit to the cave. Early visitors descended into the cave by climbing down the seventy-five foot wooden ladder to the cave waterfall. But, Hugo thought, it would be much nicer if visitors could walk along a concrete trail lighted with electric lights. But, establishing a path through the cave would require carrying a multitude of heavy sacks of cement down the entrance ladder. Jack Herschend, a man of slight build, recalls the year the pathway was built. "Hugo was adamant that

Neighborhood square dances were often held at Marvel Cave. Here Chick Allen, Bob Mabe and others perform.

I go to college, but I could see no future in going to college. I was insistent; I wanted to stay in the Ozarks and help build the family business. Finally, Hugo agreed, and then he said, Why don't you become the gopher for the men working down in the bottom of the cave mixing the concrete and laying out the path? My job, from June through December, became that of allowing workmen above ground to load a 94 pound sack of dry concrete on each of my shoulders and then helping me by placing my feet on the first rung of the ladder, which I then descended, carrying the two heavy sacks of concrete to the workmen below. After climbing down that ladder to the waterfall and removing the sacks from my shoulder, the return trip to the top to get more sacks was a piece of cake." But the "gopher work" also motivated Jack to go to college. Is it any wonder that before year's end, Jack was eager to pack his clothes and other worldly belongings and head off to Northwestern University? He graduated three years later before returning to the family business and eventually becoming president of the family corporation.

Disaster struck the family in 1955 when Hugo suffered his second heart attack and died. At the time both boys were away from home, Jack in the military, and Peter at college. It became Mary's task to head the fledgling family business, located underneath a rough Ozark hillside. What a formidable task! Why not just return to family and friends in Chicago?

But Mary was determined to stay and run the new business. She felt at home in the Ozarks, wanted to fulfill her husband's visions for the property, and had the knack of tending to the details necessary for running a business. Her inspiration to continue with the new venture came from the tenacious character of the two Lynch sisters she had succeeded at Marvel Cave. When her two sons reaffirmed their decision to return, Mary continued her unremitting efforts to build the family business.

One of Mary's first decisions was to complete another of her husband's plans for the interior of the cave, namely to build a tramway to take visitors out of the cave. By 1957 the Herschends were ready to begin the arduous work. Jack served as the chief engineer of the project. He began by mapping the cave to find the most advantageous place to drill a tunnel to the surface. After weeks of exploration, he and the cave guides decided the nearest place was in Blondie's Throne, a 94 foot dome pit. The distance to the surface was 267 feet through solid rock. For the next several months Jack spent his evenings setting dynamite charges and blasting the rock, then, with the workmen's help, his days carrying the huge boulders from the ever-lengthening passageway. One near-tragic mishap occurred on

Main Street Silver Dollar City

the first trial run of the train when Jack, eager to test the operation of the cable train, attempted to ride the train down the new tracks—only to discover the cable to the train had not been connected. The train slammed into the limestone wall at the end of the cave, hurling Jack into the rock wall. Although seriously injured with broken bones to one leg, crushed disks, and 57 stitches, Jack recovered sufficiently to attend the dedication of the train on May 11, 1958. And, proving that they already had an eye for publicity, they enlisted Casey Jones, Jr., son of the subject of the ballad, to help initiate the maiden trip up the steep hillside. With the railroad in operation, the development of the cave was complete.

The Herschends immediately began to search for ways to expand their growing attraction. Though Hugo had once hinted that an Ozark village would be a worthy endeavor, Peter Herschend gives Russell Pearson credit for putting the idea in motion. Pearson was a carnival man who lived his life dreaming of ways to entertain people. He had already helped build one "old west" town, Frontier City, in Oklahoma City. Arriving at Marvel Cave on Labor Day, in 1958, unknown and uninvited, he proposed to the Herschends that they rejuvenate the idea, first fostered by Hugo, of building an old Ozark Village where the past could be relived.

The Herschends connected Pearson's idea with the almost forgotten town of Marble City. Pearson's sketch, an old Ozark village, included five stores at seven-eighths scale facing a wide main street where old time Ozark music, contests, and mock family feuds could be held. The new village was developed to accent the activities of the cave and draw visitors to the underground cavern. Mary Herschend studied the sketches, made several modifications, and then approved the building plans. She wanted to assure herself that every inch of her buildings would resemble an 1890 Ozark Main Street. In a kind of environmental impact statement years ahead of its time, she insisted that during construction the landscape be altered as little as possible. She was adamant that no trees would be removed, other than those that absolutely interfered with the construction of a building. When her two sons committed themselves to remaining with the family business rather than setting out on their own, the trio set to work.

The first public notice of the Herschends efforts appeared in the October 15, 1959 edition of the Stone County Republican newspaper in an article that quoted Mary Herschend announcing the imminent construction of an 1800's Ozark Village near the entrance to Marvel Cave. The notice outlined the building of homes, a church, general store, mill, livery stable, print shop, and photo gallery. Construction of the village, she announced, was to be under the supervision of Mr. Russell Pearson of Oklahoma City.

Later in the year, although the date is difficult to ascertain, Mary Herschend hosted area newspaper reporters to further discuss plans for the new village. At what today would be called a press conference, Bob Mabe was invited to bring his band to play for friends and reporters. Bob readily agreed,

A native craftsman, white oak basket maker Leslie Jones, was recruited to demonstrate his trade at Silver Dollar City.

using the name Baldknobbers for the first time. When the band, consisting of Bob, and his brothers Jim, Bill, Lyle, and his then father in law, Chick Allen, arrived, they brought not just their fiddles and guitars but a host of native instruments, a washtub, washboard, a crosscut saw, and a novelty instrument for keeping time to the music, an old jawbone of a mule, that Chick played. They called the instrument a jacksassaphone.

Thus, amidst the excitement of the day, not one but two Branson institutions were spawned, Silver Dollar City and, since the Baldknobbers became the first music show in Branson, a whole new musical industry. Eventually, the Baldknobbers would be followed in Branson by hundreds of bands and thousands of musicians and entertainers, some nationally known stars who had received multiple national honors for their talent and abilities. In a town that soon became quite adept at scheduling press conferences, this one, the first, was the most important press conference ever held in Branson. But, no one that day could have anticipated the kind of future that lay ahead for either of the ventures. Certainly, both the Herschends of Silver Dollar City and the Mabes of the Baldknobbers were concerned about their short-term future, with keeping their economic heads above water. They did not want to go broke.

The two followed separate, although occasionally over the years, intertwining, paths. For years, the growth of Silver Dollar City far outstripped that of the music industry. Almost from the start, locals sensed that the attraction would bring visitors and perhaps prosperity to the placid Branson area. Workmen from neighboring towns converged on the City, eager to construct the buildings on Main Street. Soon performers and artisans mixed with the workers, building not just a town, but an entertainment center where visitors would be welcomed and entertained, with the anticipation that they would purchase locally made craft items before they departed.

From the beginning, the Wilderness Church mirrored the religious beliefs of the Herschend family.

The Herschends give Don Richardson, their public relations manager and former director of publicity for the recently cancelled Ozark Jubilee television show out of Springfield, credit for naming Silver Dollar City. With the knowledge that "word of-mouth" advertising was "the best kind" of advertising, the founders, at Don's suggestion, just three weeks before opening day, decided to name the village Silver Dollar City. With their limited advertising budget they believed that, when making change, they would give customers real silver dollar coins as exchange for purchases. Thus, it was hoped that visitors would pass the dollars on to others throughout the area, triggering a chain reaction that would publicize the park. The ploy soon failed as an advertising gimmick, but the name Silver Dollar City stuck and remains to this day the name of the theme park.

Jack, Mary and Peter in front of an early favorite ride, the Silver Dollar City Stagecoach.

Two weeks before the opening, the Herschends were still out scouring the Ozark countryside, recruiting native Ozark craftsmen to demonstrate their crafts at the City.

Opening day for Silver Dollar City was May 1, 1960. There was plenty for everyone to do. Guests could ride sure-footed donkeys, pet the mules, watch the construction of a full sized Conestoga wagon, see blacksmith Shad Heller hammer out souvenirs over a hot bellowing forge at a blacksmith shop, and observe woodcarver Peter Engler carve intricate, museum quality masterpieces. Clerks in the old-time stores waited on customers. And, every hour on the hour, turmoil was created near the cave entrance on Main Street when the Hatfields and McCoys staged a mock gunfight charging at each other from different directions, poised to raise a hullabaloo in front of guests. It was hoped that after the ruckus, visitors would purchase tickets for the cave tour, the only fee charged at Silver Dollar City at the time. And, the Baldknobber band returned to entertain guests.

The response from visitors the first year exceeded expectations. The Herschends discovered to their surprise that they were not in the cave touring business after all. They had become theme park managers.

From the beginning the expansion of Silver Dollar City has proceeded on a nearly continuous basis. During the early years, the Herschends planned building projects for the wintertime so that the entertainers and craftsmen could help construct the year's project, giving employees year round work.

To keep the theme of the Ozarks alive in the Park, the Herschends next found and moved two existing log buildings to the main street. The first building was the McHaffie Homestead. The cabin was real and had weathered Taney County storms for years, but at the time was threatened by the backwaters of Lake Bull Shoals. It was moved, piece by piece, to Silver Dollar City. The second log building, the abandoned Wilson Creek schoolhouse, had been used by local school children for years. At Silver Dollar City the building was converted to a church and the pulpit was fashioned by one of the laborers from a huge Oak tree, one of the few removed during the construction of Main Street. The church continues to this day to reflect the values of the founders of the City.

The next addition, a railroad, The Frisco Silver Dollar City Line, was constructed to carry visitors from the edge of the city, circle through the woods, and return back to the station. Because the original engine could not make the entire run without running out of steam, staff at Silver Dollar City created a mock raid at the bottom of the hill to stop the train and entertain the passengers while the engineer rebuilt the needed head of steam. The ruffians, the Alf Bolin Gang, named for an early band of local outlaws, have become a permanent part of train trips at Silver Dollar City and continue to this day their clumsy, entertaining, but never-successful attempts to rob the train. Other attractions—a new restaurant, pottery shop, and general store—followed in quick succession as the town expanded down the hill. Finally, a flour mill and bakery, named Sullivan's Mill for a man who gave an old miller's stone and waterwheel to the Herschends, completed the second phase. Visitors could watch the slow turning of belts, shafts, and gears transform grain into flour—and smell the aroma of fresh-baked bread.

Both Herschend brothers give Andy Miller credit for being "the theme conscience" of Silver Dollar City. Andy had formerly been the set designer on the stage of the Ozark Jubilee. At the demise of the Jubilee, the Herschends recruited him as a designer for the Silver Dollar City developments. Andy's job was not just to fashion each building, but to monitor the authenticity of the 1880's theme, rendering it cohesively throughout the park and carrying the theme through in all publicity. Much of his work from these early years is still evident on the park today.

But, the Herschends realized it wasn't just the souvenir or the product or the craft that visitors craved. Guests wanted an experience; something special, a joyful memory of their day's visit that they could go home and talk about—an experience to share with others. Thus, when Walker Powell, the grandson of one of the civil war veterans that incorporated the early Marble City and an early employee of the park was tagged to become the park "cheese maker", the Herschends teamed him with a pretty and spirited young native, Karlene Norman, to work beside him and sell the cheese. Karlene held visitors attention with exaggerated tales of her old unruly Jersey cow that she had to milk by hand each morning to get the milk to give to Walker to make the cheese the park visitors would eat. Visitors gathered around the cheese shop to listen to the audacious stories she told about herself and her Jersey cow—and to purchase cheese. It was the experience that really mattered.

From the beginning, Silver Dollar City encouraged "street characters" employees who exuded charisma, an extra smile, who enjoyed the company of others while being a bit eccentric, to give life to the park. One was the city's blacksmith and mayor, Shad Heller, an actor by training, who kept his office at the forge near the park entrance. Shad and woodcarving shopkeeper Peter Engler, a world-class woodcarver, kept a continuous feud going in front of park guests. When Peter passed the forge on his way to work, he would complain bitterly about the pot holes in the street. Shad would respond about the ungrateful residents of the city, then mutter something about releasing a bag full of termites in the woodcarving shop. Shakespeare-quoting John Corbin made iron-runged wagon wheels, sang in the variety shows, and, during the off-season, served as the park plumber. The street characters added to the experience of park visitors.

While Jack Herschend took the lead in park construction and management, Peter recognized the need for marketing. Showing an uncanny instinct for publicity, Peter would hustle local craftsmen dressed in hill country garb—basket makers, potters, woodcarvers, the blacksmith, and soap maker—into a small company-owned van and speed them off to live noontime television shows in surrounding major cities: Springfield, Kansas City, St. Louis, Tulsa, Omaha, Ft. Smith, Memphis, even as far away as Chicago. Wherever he could get a TV booking, for up to twelve weeks a year, six weeks in the springtime and six before the fall season,

The rambunctious feud of the Hatfields and McCoys ignited hourly on main street.

Above: Live, noon television shows were popular for Silver Dollar City street characters. Here Chick Allen dances a jig. Shad Heller and Violet Hensley are playing in the background.

Left: Chick Allen and Peter Herschend share a moment off stage.

Peter would take his entourage of local craftsmen. From the beginning, it was obvious that television audiences enjoyed seeing Ozark craftsmen making native crafts, for attendance at Silver Dollar City climbed steadily upward.

The two brothers developed an excellent working relationship, each with a unique ability that complimented the other's skill. That relationship extended even into the conduct of early church services at the park. Jack relates that from the beginning, Sunday morning services were offered at the Silver Dollar City chapel with area pastors contacted to fill the pulpit. Although scheduled well in advance of their appointments, some ministers still failed to show. Yet the services had been announced, worshippers were in the pews, and services had to be conducted. In anticipation that this might happen, the brothers often listened to Billy Graham revivals on television the night before and, when a guest minister failed to show, the two would flip a coin. The winner would lead the congregation in singing for ten minutes, giving the other time to prepare a sermon–no doubt a warmed-over Billy Graham delivery, which he would then give to the expectant audience. Surely, God was watching over this pair.

Nor were Mary Herschend's efforts in the growth of the business overlooked. To local workers, she was known as a fierce champion of the City. Her contributions were recognized in 1968 by the state of Missouri when the Federal Small Business Administration honored her as Missouri Small Businessman of the Year, a term that today would be regarded as politically incorrect. The award brought satisfaction to her family although they were amused that the family matriarch was called a "businessman." Four years later, in 1972, she received the first Missouri Tourism Award for her contributions to tourism throughout the state. Also in 1972, she was paired with Mary Trimble to receive a "first-ev-

The Medicine Show Quartet: Shad Heller, Colonel Ray, Peter Herschend and John Corbin

The cast of the Beverly Hillbillies on Main Street in 1969.

er" Branson Chamber of Commerce award, that of honoring a Branson resident for their service to the betterment of the Branson community. The Chamber then named the award the Mary Award after the two women. The award continues to be the most prestigious award given each winter at the annual Branson Chamber black-tie dinner.

The culminating event of the early years came in the summer of 1969 when the wildly popular national TV show, the Beverly Hillbillies, moved cast, technicians, and props to the City for a summer filming of five episodes.

The show was a cornball spoof about a family of lovable hill people who had struck it rich and moved to Hollywood. The characters in the show—Granny, Jed, Jethro, and Ellie Mae—pursued their simple needs with an energetic lifestyle that contrasted sharply with the ostentatious living of Hollywood. The show was brought to Silver Dollar City because Don Richardson proposed to Paul Henning, producer of the television show, that the Beverly Hillbillies should have a real home in the Ozark hills. The plot was hatched when Granny decided to find a boyfriend for the young and vivacious Ellie Mae, and Granny was certain no boy in all of Hollywood would be acceptable for her granddaughter. Only a "country boy" would do for a boyfriend. Thus, the family moved to Silver Dollar City to find an acceptable suitor.

Area newspapers were full of the news. Autographed pictures of the TV stars plastered the walls of local restaurants. Silver Dollar City employees lined up to be extras in the shows. Crowds gathered to watch the filming, and Silver Dollar City blacksmith, Shad Heller, became an instant favorite in homes across America. At the conclusion of the filming, Ellie Mae, although she did not find a permanent boyfriend, told visitors at the set about her enjoyable visit to Silver Dollar City. On the final day of filming, the stars feted the workers at Silver Dollar City to an evening dinner.

The national exposure ushered in an era of near miraculous growth for the small family- owned theme park. Gate receipts spiraled upward. The park grew further down the hill and into the holler. The huge glass blowing furnace was installed, followed in successive years by the Ozark Marketplace, saloon, courthouse, diving bell, and Tom Sawyer's Landing. Additional restaurants were added and the music festivals begun. In just a few short years, the park doubled in size.

In 1967 Jack and Peter Herschend made what was probably their most farsighted decision in the management history of the company when they attended a meeting of the American Management Association. Here they listened to some of America's foremost corporate leaders talking about the responsibilities of corporate ownership. By the following year, the two brothers had incorporated Silver Dollar City, with Jack becoming President, and Peter, vice-president. In the process, they added an outside board of directors to the company. The decision provided a corporate structure that added strength to their efforts and flexibility for the growth that was to follow.

The Herschends were on their way to developing America's largest family owned entertainment corporation, Herschend Family Enterprises. Silver Dollar City had become a monumental success.

Branson Music Pioneers
The First Four Shows

The Baldknobbers

When the Mabe Brothers walked into the community room underneath the city hall of Branson for their first music show in 1960, they did not even bother with sound equipment. The room would only seat about 50 people and, with a nonexistent stage, they simply stood at the front of the room and played their music. The four Mabe brothers, Bob, Bill, Lyle, and Jim, had already performed at Plum Nelly Days and several other Branson festivals, at the downtown Jim Owens theater, at the press conference announcing Silver Dollar City, and again the following year at the opening day of the new theme park. At the time of their first show, they were cast members of the Shepherd of the Hills Drama just west of Branson, outside the city limits just beyond Dewey Bald Mountain. They had already picked a name for themselves, The Baldknobbers, referencing an area vigilante group formed in the latter part of the 1880's, in the aftermath of the Civil War. The original vigilante Baldknobbers had, at first, brought law and order to the anarchy of the county, but in short order had turned lawless themselves. Stories of the vigilante's activities still circulated in the county in 1960.

The Baldknobbers, the musical group, were well enough known throughout the community that, had they so wanted, they could have played at one of the Branson night clubs to late-night Friday and Saturday audiences, where many of the locals gathered on the weekends to relax and dance, socialize, and drink beer. The night clubs, the Allendale on the lakefront, the Log Jam on Highway 248, or the Fireside on Gretna Road, were available to them. Instead, they set their sights on something bigger. They modeled their show after the well known country music shows of the era, the Barn Dance of WLS, Chicago, the Midwestern Hayride of WLW, Cincinnati, the Louisiana Hayride of KWKH, Shreveport, and the most famous of them all, the Grand Ole Opry of WSM, Nashville. The Mabe Brothers wanted a show where, as entertainers, they could romp around on a stage and play and sing and dance and tell jokes and entertain while audience members clapped their hands, stomped their feet, hooted and howled, and sang along.

But there was another show, almost in their own backyard, that influenced the Mabes more

Pictured above is Red Foley and announcer Joe Slattery on the set of the Ozark Jubilee. The Jubilee has had a long running impact on the Branson music scene. The prduction was broadcast from the Jewell Theatre in downtown Springfield.

than the radio country music shows. That show, the Ozark Jubilee, the first televised Country Music Show in the nation, was broadcast out of Springfield. Although recently cancelled, the Ozark Jubilee had completed an unbelievably successful five year run. The Jubilee was the joint product of television station KY3-TV and radio station KWTO, and featured national country music recording star Red Foley as the emcee. Country music stars of the period clamored to be on the show, and emerging artists received tremendous boosts from appearances. The presence of the many country music stars nearby inspired their efforts.

It took considerable prodding from Bob for all of the brothers to agree to join a live show. Never before had anyone presented such a show in Branson. However, Bob urged his brothers on, telling them that "if you'll just stick with me, we can make $200.00 a week" and, when he found that the community room in the basement of city hall could be rented, they agreed to the evening performances. When they recruited their wives to stand on street corners waving to tourists with home made signs advertising the show, the Baldknobbers knew they would receive the family support they needed. They publicized their show as The Baldknobbers Hillbilly Jamboree Stage Show.

That first performance marked the beginning of the first continuous running music show in Branson. The show consisted of all four brothers with Bob as the band manager and emcee. Lyle, as the comedian George Aggernite, played the washtub. Jim, who had developed a second comic routine for the group, called himself "Droopy Drawers," and played the washboard, while Bill played the dobro. All four sang. Chick Allen played the "bones" and jig danced and Delbert Howard played the fiddle. It was an unconventional band.

The Mabe brothers grew up in Nixa, Missouri, a crossroads town just south of Springfield. The family was a large one, with eleven surviving children, six boys and five girls. Two other children had died in infancy. The family had been raised on a hardscrabble Ozark farm where their father, Donald, looked after the upkeep of the farm, making certain fences were kept up, the barn in repair, and the milk cows in good health. For added income he drove a school bus morning and night and became a minister, dividing his time between two half-time pastorates in small, nearby churches. He was the overseer of the family.

It was mother's task to raise the children and look after the daily chores on the farm. Mother Hazel organized her brood carefully; each child looked after the next youngest and each had a chore to do each day. As the Mabes raised most of their own food, there was the family garden to tend, and the dozen milk cows to be milked twice each day. For meat, a hog was butchered each fall and the hams and bacons cured, salted, and put away until winter. Everyone pitched in to make the family as self sufficient as possible. And, when possible, Hazel would send the newborn calves to the local auction barn each year for extra spending money.

Often it was left to the older sister, Pauline, to bandage the cuts, hurts, and bruises that farm kids accumulate--and to kiss their small hurts away. In the Mabe family, prayer preceded each meal and Mom made certain all children attended the nearby Highlandville Baptist Church three times each week, on Sunday morning and Sunday night, and for Wednesday night prayer meetings. The family found strength in religion.

The Mabes could aptly be described as "dirt-poor." Later in life the boys acknowledged, "we were poor growing up, but we just didn't know it," as were many other Ozark natives of that generation.

The Mabe children found an outlet for their youthful energy when one day, perhaps by accident, one of the boys found an old rusty hand saw back in a darkened corner of the milk barn. That old saw unleashed their first musical talent, for they already knew that old saws were used by comedians as a novelty to bring variety to stage shows. They had seen stage performers make music by bending a saw back on itself in a tight curve and then pull a horsehair fiddle bow across the taut blade. Bob and Bill experimented with the old saw around the farm house, at first getting a few squawking sounds, then recognizable notes, and finally a couple of tunes to country music songs. The old saw kept them occupied for days, and it boosted their confidence. They discovered that, with persistence, they could flush out musical tunes.

Older sister Pauline supplied the first real musical instrument the boys ever owned, an old guitar with one string missing. Pauline attended a nearby neighborhood auction, and while there bid on an old dilapidated three-string guitar. After placing the winning bid, she took the old guitar home to the boys. The enthusiastic boys quickly taught themselves to play the thing. First they tuned it like a dobro, in a G chord, and then slid a knife along the strings to produce the melody. Then, for music, they listened to country stations on the radio, and soon developed a repertoire of songs.

A short time later a family neighbor, Earl Blanset, showed up at the house with a fully-intact guitar, offering it to the financially hard-strapped boys for $35.00. Earl, however, extended them credit for the $35.00. Bob, in particular, took a liking to the guitar and practiced constantly. Soon Bob and the guitar became almost inseparable. He was on his way to becoming a musician. Over the years the $35.00 loan, although never repaid, became a running joke between Bob and Earl.

Bob, the oldest of the brothers, became the music organizer of the Mabe family. Before long, Bob, along with his brothers and sister Margie, were singing at Sunday worship services and Sunday afternoon church sings. They were asked to sing at fox hunts, which were popular at the time. At the hunts, the hunters gathered at forest edges early in the afternoons with their hounds. Waiting for dark, the hunters spent their afternoons talking about their hounds and telling hunting stories—and listening to a band play music—before turning their own hounds loose to trail a fox.

The hunters enjoyed the baying of the hounds—the ringing cry of the hounds on the trail of a fox—perhaps even more than the music of the Mabes. A good fox hunter could pick out the cry of his own dog in a pack of hounds on the chase. They could pull from the chorus of the hounds the sound of the dog in the lead of the pack and which was tiring, and falling behind. Yet, by late night or early morning, everyone would be tired, the hunters would call in their dogs, and all could go home. And, at fox hunts, the fox was never killed. The fox was always left to run another time. The Mabes would be home long before the fox entered its own den.

For a short period of time Bob performed in a country band led by a Springfield policeman, Buck Tindle, who became famous when, in the course of his police duties, he captured a truck load of cobra snakes that had escaped from an overturned truck passing through Springfield. Tindle's feat earned him a cover picture on "Life" magazine in 1953.

Bob's final music job in Springfield was to play a 15 minute early morning radio show as part of The Blansit Trio, with sister Margie, who by then was Mrs. Wilbur Blansit, and Hollis Warren. The group was sponsored by Wilbur and Earl Blansit who were auctioneers and owned a cattle auction sale barn at nearby Ozark. The Blansits used the show to publicize their cattle sales to the farmers in the listening area who might need either to buy or sell their livestock. The Blansits morning show was one of several 15 minute live music shows on the dominant radio station of the Ozarks, KWTO. (During this period of time one KWTO producer replaced Chet Atkins in favor of a young, mellow-voiced butcher from West Plains, Porter Wagoner.)

And, at KWTO Bob met an old time Ozark fiddler, Lonnie Robertson, and his wife, Thelma, who still played the traditional music the early Scot settlers brought with them into the Ozarks. The

Chick Allen, Bob, Lyle, and Jim Mabe and Ray Bruffet, playing at the opening of Silver Doller City. This guest appearance helped solidify the Baldknobbers.

Above: Lyle (George Aggernite) and wife Betty Mabe on opening day.

Bob Mabe

Robertsons, although still Ozark favorites, were in the waning years of their entertainment careers. On two occasions Bob and the Robertsons teamed up for public performances, once at Eldorado Springs, Missouri, and the other time at Bakersville. For each performance, Bob piled into the back seat of Robertson's '47 Chrysler and rode with them to the performance. Bob emceed the shows and sang his favorite songs at the time, "Mocking Bird Hill" and "King of the Road" before introducing Lonnie and Thelma, who entertained with their traditional fiddle music. One wonders if any of the audience members on those nights realized they were seeing, side by side on the program, one of the last of the popular traditional Ozark entertainers and one of the new rising stars in the business.

Throughout the 1950's Bob Mabe was paying his dues as a musician, even as he worked his day job as a salesman with the Hageman Tobacco Company in Springfield.

The early shows extended their seasons with wintertime touring.
These coaches show the increasing prosperity of the Baldknobbers over the years.

But it was Lyle Mabe, the comedian of the group, who became the early celebrity of the family. Lyle discovered his comedic abilities in Branson in the early 1950's when Bob was invited to appear at the Owens movie theater in downtown Branson. Bob enlisted his sister Margie and brother Lyle to help with the performance. Margie brought a pet along, a small, white dog, and even had the young animal on stage beside her. Bob asked her the name of the animal and it was Lyle who responded, "Why, it's Spot." The audience chuckled and Lyle discovered he had comic appeal. Before long he took the stage name George Aggernite, began dressing in outlandish hillbilly garb, and developed his own skits. Shortly thereafter, he landed a spot on Springfield television station KYTV advertising for a local gas company, Empire Gas, out of Lebanon, Missouri. Buffooning the gas company, Aggernite mumbled and fumbled his way through each commercial but was never, in the course of several years of advertising, able to pronounce the word 'economical', a word that appeared at the end of each of his ads. Viewers of the commercials looked forward to seeing Aggernite again mispronounce the word, making him a celebrity to the TV listening audience and gaining customers for the gas company.

In 1958, when radio station KWTO went to an all record format and replaced their staff musicians with a chattering disk jockey, the Blansit Trio was a part of that change. The Trio left the station without a radio program and Bob again without a musical job.

Bob was overjoyed the following year when Jack Herschend called and asked him to bring a band to the press conference that announced the opening of Silver Dollar City. He was even more ecstatic when the following spring, just two weeks before the opening of the City, Jack again called, but this time asked him if he could play a banjo at the actual opening day. The request caused consternation. Bob did not even own a banjo and he certainly had never played one. "Well, you have two weeks to learn to play one, then," responded Jack with a laugh. The following day Bob purchased a five string banjo from a Springfield pawn shop, and in two weeks, along with his brothers, was doing creditably well playing the banjo at the opening of Silver Dollar City. The band played for guests all day long at the opening of the park, gaining valuable local recognition for the name, the Baldknobbers.

The Baldknobbers performed at the Sammy Lane Pavilion near the waterfront in Branson.

Bob was even more enthusiastic when Mark Trimble also called in the winter of 1959 and asked if the Balknobbers would be a part of the new Shepherd of the Hills Drama that would be performed nightly. It took the brothers little time to agree to the job. They would actually get a regular paycheck for acting in the drama and playing their music. It meant they could keep the band together.

By the fall of 1960, they were seasoned musicians with the eagerness of youth on their side and ready to try their own show. But there was no road map to follow, no one before them had charted the course for Branson. No wonder they were apprehensive. Still, they believed the time was ripe to try the new venture. With Bob's urging, the Baldknobbers made the historic decision. Within two years they were able to leave the Shepherd of the Hills pageant and concentrate solely on their downtown show. However, at this point, they still had their day jobs.

The Mabes tell stories about having only sixteen people show up for one of their early performances, but they went on with the show anyway, jammin' and talking to their guests, including them in the show. One couple in attendance, an Iowa couple, ended up becoming good friends and over the years brought several bus loads of visitors to Baldknobber performances. Another time, a particularly begrudging old gentleman sat on the front row and noticeably never even cracked a smile throughout the entire performance. After the show, he walked up to Bob and said, "That's the best show I've ever seen," On another occasion Chick Allen insisted on fulfilling his routine in the show, jig dancing, two different times, even though he had a badly cracked rib. Ouch. But, the show must go on.

Tourists quickly deemed the Baldknobbers worthy of an evening of entertainment during their vacation stay in Branson and so their reputation as a guitar pickin', joke tellin', fun-lovin' group of young men quickly turned into box office sales. Soon, they were seeking larger auditoriums. From the initial room at city hall, the Baldknobbers moved to the 200 seat Sammy Lane Pavilion near the waterfront. Then, one day, Bob noticed the owner of the skating rink near the lake with hammer and crowbar in hand, getting ready to tear the old building down. On the spot, the two negoti-

A converted skating rink served as the first music theatre in Branson.

ated a $1600 price for the building and Branson had its first theater, a converted old skating rink which seated 500 people.

At the time, tourist season coincided with fishing season, from early April until late October. To lengthen their season, the Mabes purchased a bus and traveled during the winter months to out-of-town playing dates. The first van, a white '64 Ford, could haul all the sound equipment and still seat 6 people. It was a practice later followed by many of the other bands in Branson. They too, purchased vans and buses for out-of-town winter dates.

In a couple of years all the brothers had quit their day jobs in Springfield.

Finally in 1969, nine years after they began in Branson, the Baldknobbers purchased a 14 acre plot on Highway 76 and built an 865 seat theater–a theater which has been expanded twice and now seats 1,700 people. Before long they were booking Nashville stars, including many who had only recently performed at the Ozark Jubilee in Springfield. Barbara Mandrell, Porter Waggoner and Dolly Parton, Mel Tillis, and Ernest Tubbs were among their guests. The guest appearances were important in introducing the entertainers to Branson, for Dolly Parton would eventually build a Dolly Parton Dixie Stampede in Branson, Mel Tillis his own, huge theater on Highway 248 north of town, and Barbara Mandrell would make regular guests appearances at the Grand Palace.

The Baldknobbers persevered and in so doing, thrived. Their efforts were rewarded with success, paving the way for the musical industry that would follow.

The Presleys' Country Jubilee

In the mid 1930's, ten year old Lloyd Presley's older brother, Don, traded his best hound dog to a neighbor for a beat up old guitar. Brother Don didn't take much to the guitar, so Lloyd picked it up and started picking out a few tunes he had heard on the radio. The pickin' "took" and Lloyd just kept on learning more songs and performing whenever he had a chance. It was the beginning of a career that carried into several generations of Presleys and greatly influenced what Branson has become today.

Like the Mabe family of the Baldknobbers, the musical journey of the Presleys centered around Springfield, church, pie suppers, fox hunts, country music, and the radio and television stations of Springfield, Missouri. For Lloyd, who became the patriarch of the family, the actual beginning started in Brighton, Missouri, a crossroads town just a few miles north of Springfield. When his brother, Don, tired of that old guitar and handed it over to him, Lloyd was quick to learn the basics of guitar playing. Another brother, Elwin learned to play the guitar and mother played the harmonica. Soon the family was ready to climb up on farm wagons at pie suppers, fox hunts, and Sunday gospel sings, tapping their toes and singing and strumming the tunes they had taught themselves. These first Plummer family music shows were an early portend of things to come.

By the mid '40's Lloyd was taking time out from his "day time" job of delivering produce around Spingfield. He began playing with a group called the Ozark Playboys on the first ever radio station in Springfield, KGBX. By the early fifties the band was touring on Saturday afternoons to the small farm towns throughout the Ozarks with the Loyd Evans farm show out of radio station KWTO Springfield. Loyd Evans was the farm director of the station and through a "Farm Show" the farm director hoped to capitalize on the shopping habits of farm people whose custom at the time was to congregate at their nearest town on Saturday afternoons and evenings to shop and visit with neighbors. Loyd figured that by taking some entertainment to a different small community each Saturday, he could build up goodwill for the radio station, as well as make some extra money for both himself and the entertainers. Thus, he invited the Ozark Playboys, a band that included Bill and Jim and Windy Luttrell as well as Lloyd Presley to accompany him out to the busy Ozark communities for a Saturday afternoon of fun and entertainment.

When the Ozark Jubilee began production in Springfield, the broadcasting facilities experienced "technological difficulties" and Red Foley and the cast were forced to travel to an uplink site in Columbia, Missouri, for three months in order to transmit the show onto the national airwaves. The Ozark Playboys, including guitar picker Lloyd Presley, was picked to substitute for the cast to play at the Jewell Theater.

In the early 1960's Lloyd again teamed up to perform in another of Loyd Evans roadshows, this one called the "Farmarama." Farmarama performances were broadcast on Saturday nights from a cave called Fantastic Caverns north of Springfield. At the time, the cave was owned by the man whose family also owned the Shepherd of the Hills Homestead, Mark Trimble. For the first time, but certainly not the last, the lives of the two young entrepreneurs intertwined.

Fantastic Caverns was important not just for Lloyd, but also for his son, Gary, who as a teenager at the time, was just beginning to perform on stage. (Gary's first public appearance occurred when he was four years old. His father had hoisted him up on a chair in front of a microphone at radio station KGBX where he sang "Rudolph the Red Nosed Reindeer.") In need of comedy for his act at Fantastic Caverns, Loyd Evans asked Gary to "just make 'em laugh." Gary, a natural comedian, began cutting up on stage until he had developed his own character, Herkimer, a flamboyant, energetic, "off-the-wall" Ozark Hillbilly. The character Herkimer added needed variety to the show and eventually became the trademark of the Presleys' Country Jubilee. The Presley tradition of multiple family members on stage had begun.

There was one more stop for the Presley family, another cave, before they settled into a theater in Branson. This venue was Herman Mead's Underground Theater, fifteen miles west of Branson. The cave featured a large cavern suitable for an auditorium, and with the natural air conditioning of the earth it was ideal for attracting customers on blistering hot summer days.

One of Lloyd's friends, Bob White, who produced the shows, was able to entice his musical friends down from Springfield, many of them former stars on the Ozark Jubilee. Slim Wilson, Speedy Haworth, and even Red Foley appeared at Herman Mead's Underground Theater. His list of performers included Gary Presley, who, as Herkimer, provided comedy while his younger sister Janice sang country songs. Lloyd, too, joined his children on stage. The family's musical tradition grew and the cave served the Presleys well, except, occasionally, while on stage, performers would hear the sound of a 22 shot at the back of the auditorium. Upon investigation, they discovered it was Herman, firing his pistol at an occasional rat that tried to invade the refreshment stand during show time. The cave was also the training ground for the little shaver, Steve Presley, Lloyd's youngest son, who hung around the refreshment stand helping Herman's wife, Merle, serve coffee, soda pop, cake, and donuts.

Family life placed Lloyd in Branson. In 1942 young Lloyd began frequenting the skating rink at Doling Park in Springfield, not so much because he enjoyed roller skating, but because of the pretty young girl he had met there. She was Bessie Mae Garrison from Alpena Pass, Arkansas, a small town just over the state line, south of Branson. She was the love of his life, and the marriage that soon followed lasted 64 years, until her death in 2007. With the marriage, the Presley tradition of "family" began, for both Lloyd and Bessie Mae had already developed a strong religious faith that included a deep sense of family commitment. From the beginning, these ideals have remained the lifelong guideposts for the family entertainment business that was soon to follow.

Passing through Branson on family trips to Alpena Pass acquainted Lloyd with the town. Living in Branson would shorten the trip to Alpena. Plus, Branson had other advantages, too. Lloyd loved to fish and already was guiding fishing expeditions on the new Table Rock Lake. He developed a plan to implement his new lifestyle—fishing and making music. For work, he could guide tourists on the new lake and even, because of his connections with Springfield television stations, give a weekly fishing report on Table Rock Lake. For music he began talking with a Springfield builder, Larry Drennon, a country music fan, about building a theater in Branson, this one out west of town, on Highway 76.

Lloyd and Larry soon decided there was room for another theater. "With so many tourists coming into the area, how could we fail," they wondered aloud. Before long, Lloyd had called a famillly conference to solidify the decision. All family members agreed. (Besides, all realized that if the show was not a success, the building could be converted to a wintertime storage area for fishing boats that fishermen might want to leave in the area.)

The women of the family came to the financial rescue when Bessie Mae found a job with the local utility company and Pat Presley, Gary's new wife, found employment at Security Bank, downtown. It was time to take the plunge. Eight members of the Drennon and Presley families, Larry and his wife Francis, Lloyd and Bessie Mae, Gary and Pat, and the soon to be married Presley daughter, Deanna to the Drennon's son, David, signed the bank note leading to the construction of the theater.

The Presleys move to Branson resulted in the first music show that became the strip.

Cast members for the show included the Presleys, Lloyd, Gary, Janice, and Steve and the two newlyweds, David and Deanna (Presley) Drennon, Jim Luttrell and Howard Farmer. Spouses of the performers sold tickets, ushered, and kept the financial books. The theater, originally called the Mountain Music Theater, found life for itself in the spring of 1967, becoming the first music show on the strip and the second continuous running show in Branson. Todays Presleys' Country Jubilee evolved directly from this humble start.

The first seats for the theater were 363 canvas backed chairs purchased from Mark Trimble, some of the original seats Mark had used to start his Shepherd of the Hills Theater seven years earlier. When Mark expanded his outdoor theater, he no longer needed the chairs so he sold them to the Presleys for a dollar apiece. But, the Presleys discovered, there was a reason Mark was making the sale. Those canvas backed chairs also had canvas seats. Occasionally, during an evening performance

Eventually four generations of Presleys would appear on the stage at the same time.

the band could hear a rip and a head would disappear from the crowd. The canvas in another seat had given way.

From the start, publicity was a concern. Marketing started with young Steve, by now in grade school and the show's drummer, and his Dad, visiting the downtown area and lakeside campgrounds. Lloyd, driving the family car equipped with a portable sound system, invited guests to the evening show. Steve, meanwhile, would scamper over to the campsites and hand flyers to anyone who would take one.

It was Steve's job, in addition to being drummer for the band, to sneak out the back door of the theater during intermissions at the show and fasten the brightly colored Presleys' Ozark Country Jubilee bumper stickers onto cars parked in the show's parking lots. When he heard the band revving up for the second half, he would rush back in and begin beating the drums. (On occasion, the whole family got very good at taking them off, too, when a patron objected to the new sticker.)

There was a brief period of time early on, Lloyd and Bessie Mae told me years ago, when tickets were actually sold out of the backdoor of the farmhouse, located next door to the theater. The family would keep track of tickets sold, allowing them to set up the number of chairs needed for the evening performance. During the performance someone from the cast would shade his eyes, look out into the audience, and announce, "I see we sold every seat in the house tonight." It was show business!

Even clean-up after every performance needed a routine. The task fell to Lloyd, who had a flexible work schedule, and Steve. Much of the sweeping and dusting was done just after school, right before the two left to distribute flyers to area campgrounds. The two would need to hurry home

The first music theatre on Hwy 76

The Presleys' Rack Card: rack cards were an early popular form of advertising Branson. Today they are still distributed in convenience stores and restaurants through Missouri and surrounding states.

from the campgrounds, though. Both Lloyd and Steve needed to make the eight o'clock curtain call.

In 1968 the Presleys purchased sole ownership of the property on Highway 76; property that included ten acres, a farm house, and the theater. At the time Larry Drennon needed to remain closer to Springfield and his construction business. Deanna and David had decided to strike out on their own entertainment careers, performing first in a theater in Nixa, Missouri for a few years before moving to Eureka Springs, Arkansas and building the first theater in that town, the Pine Mountain Jubilee. The couple performed in Eureka Springs until their retirement in 2006.

Like many other shows in Branson, both at the time and throughout its history, the Presleys' Country Jubilee became a family show, not just because of its musical format, but because Lloyd and Bessie Mae relied on their religious faith and commitment to family members to guide them. Not only did Lloyd perform, but he insured that first Gary and then Steve, along with Janice and Deanna, had the same opportunity. Lloyd encouraged each family member, if they so desired, to take part in the family business.

Once the Branson theater was built, spouses became an integral part of the family business, with Pat and Bessie Mae leading the way, arriving at the theater early every night and staying until long after the last guest had departed, counting cash receipts and paying bills. Spouses, children, and soon grandchildren were pitching in to help. At times the duties of sons, wives, and children were almost interchangeable as they sold tickets, parked cars, ushered, cleaned the building, marketed, and performed.

When in the mid 1990's, the digital revolution in theater sound and lighting equipment, driven by powerful and complex programming computers was taking place, younger, non-performing Presley family members, college graduates, were ready for the task. The family involvement reached into every aspect of the family organization. At one time four generations of Presleys performed on stage. Years later Steve, looking back readily acknowledged that it was the love and respect of family members for each other that allowed the family to succeed.

In the beginning, though, it took four years for the show to make money and Gary was able to time his departure from his fulltime day job to coincide with the moment.

Over the years, the theater was enlarged seven times and the seating capacity increased from the original 363 seats to its current 1500 seats. But it was clear from the beginning that with hard work, an appreciation for each other, and a cooperative spirit, this family would succeed. It didn't diminish their chances, either, that the Presley family members were a talented group.

The Presley family opened their theater on what would become the strip in 1967. In 1969, the Baldknobbers paid a fond farewell to their home in the skating rink and built a theater on Highway 76, near the Presleys. They, too, would enlarge their new home many times over the ensuing years. The two theaters stood, facing each other on opposite sides of the highway, within a quarter of a mile of each other, enticing visitors to their shows. At first, theater managers wondered if the two shows would become a magnet to draw additional visitors to the area, or would they simply dilute the customer base already in Branson. They had little time to ponder their actions, for in 1973 Darrell and Rosie Plummer established a new theater, situated almost directly between the two. Now three theaters, a small theater row, took firm hold in Branson. Maybe, some thought, a music industry would develop to compliment the growing Silver Dollar City and Shepherd of the Hills Outdoor Drama that were already flourishing.

The Plummer Family Band at the time of their arrival in Branson.

Plummer Family Country Music Show

In 1973 The Plummer Family Country Music Show became the third music show in Branson, opening on the north side of the two lane Highway 76. The new theater stood midway between the Baldknobbers and the Presleys. Originators of the show, Darrell and Rosie Plummer, hailed from Knob Lick, Missouri, a town on the eastern fringe of the Ozarks, about 75 miles south of St. Louis. As a boy, Darrell sold vegetable garden seed to his neighbors. As a premium for excelling as a budding young salesman, Darrell was awarded a Roy Rogers guitar complete with instruction book, on how to play the instrument. Soon, Darrell had taught himself to play and by the time he was in his late teens, he had his own band, playing at neighborhood dances, pie suppers, and Sunday afternoon gospel sings. The guitar set him on his course for life.

One day when the band's regular accordion player called and said she had to miss a show, Darrell was able to find a substitute, a petite young redhead by the name of Rosie. The two married nine months later and today, after 55 years, the marriage is still a strong one. The couple set up housekeeping on another one of those small, hardscrabble Ozark hillside farms. Although Darrell worked in town, both shared farm duties, milking cows morning and night, feeding hogs and chickens and gathering eggs. It was also Rosie's job to churn the cream into butter to sell for family spending money. And, shortly after the marriage, two children, first Melody and then Randy, arrived to the young couple. Both were born with the musical talent for singing and playing musical instruments.

Even though they were living on a farm and raising a family, Darrell and Rosie found the time to play the country music they so enjoyed. Before long, they were again playing for pie suppers, dances, and gospel sings. By the end of the 1960's Darrel had the family playing regularly at a theater in Piedmont, Missouri.

When the family vacationed in Branson in early 1971, they were invited to jam on the set of the Shepherd of the Hills Outdoor Drama. Before leaving town, family members agreed Branson would be the ideal place for a Plummer Family Music Theater. Arriving back in Branson in 1972 they were soon able to realize their dream. First, they found a small, recently built theater for sale, the unrealized dream of another music producer. It took a year to assemble a cast and develop and market the new show. In May, 1973, living in a mobile home behind their newly purchased 500 seat theater, they gave their first Branson performance, the Plummer Family Music Show. Ticket costs for the first show were $2.00 for adults and $.50 for children. As an added benefit, audience members who arrived in a camper were allowed to remain overnight in the theater's parking lot for free.

It was Darrell's decision from the start that there would be no star in the show. On stage, everyone, family or band member, was an equal. The Plummers quickly learned, after a period of trial and error, to follow the format of the existing two theaters; to provide a variety show based on country music. Standard fare for the Plummer Family Show included a program of the latest country music, a gospel segment, and comedy. For comedy, the Plummers developed a lovable, but irascible Hillbilly backwoodsman, "Cousin Zeke," or Tim Cagle in real life, to bring laughter to the audience. Another performer, Harley Clements, recruited that first year to be a part of the show, performed with the Plummers for the total eighteen years they were in Branson. Another lesson learned that first year was how to remove those pesky, well-glued promotional stickers that read Plummer Family Country Music Show from the back bumpers of cars which so annoyed several of their patrons. In following years their stickers had much less adhesive.

At the early shows, bumper stickers were often attached to cars in theater parking lots.

Theatre change is a part of entertainment life in Branson. Moe Bandy was the next occupant of the theatre after the Plummers left in 1990.

In keeping with other venues in town, it took hard work, perseverance, and three years before the Plummers could call themselves a financial success. But succeed they did, expanding their theaters in a few short years to 860 seats and, as did all the shows in Branson at the time, playing mostly to overflowing crowds in the latter seventies and throughout the eighties. And, like the other Branson shows, the Plummers booked late fall and early winter dates in the northern states, first in Iowa, Nebraska, and South Dakota, and in the late wintertime in Arkansas, Louisiana, and Texas. The Plummers sold their theater to a supporter of country music stars, Moe Bandy, who then renamed the theater after one of Moe's hits, The Americana Theater. The Plummer's gave their last theater performance in October, 1990, after eighteen years of performances in Branson.

The Foggy River Boys

The Plummer Family Country Music Show was quickly followed by the fourth Branson show, the Foggy River Boys, established in 1974. Bob Hubbard was the leader of the Foggys. Bob traveled a circuitous route to get to Branson. When Bob was in the third grade. his family moved to Monett, Missouri, a town located just seventy-five miles north and west of Branson. Monett was not only an Ozark farm community, but a transportation hub as well. Highway 60 (which was main street,) ran right through the center of town, past family restaurants, clothing stores, and, at the east end of town, a feed store and cattle auction barn. The tracks of the Frisco Railroad lay just two blocks south of Main Street. The noise of traffic, either automobiles or railroads, seemed always to be heard in Monett.

Even in the third grade, Bob was already an entertainer, being the proud owner of a dummy named, appropriately, Dummy Dan. Dummy Dan was a trickster and delighted Bob's classmates when he accompanied Bob to school. Bob's musical talent was discovered by his high school teacher who heard Bob humming in the hallway one day and encouraged him to join the school chorus. Immediately the teacher placed Bob in a quartet. At that early age his life found its purpose.

By the time Bob graduated from high school in the middle '40's, he was singing in a quartet called the 4-H's, named after the group's members, Alfred Higgins, Jim Helmkamp, Culley Holt, and Hubbard. To his good fortune, just as that group disbanded in the late 40's another quartet in the Springfield area was parting ways. That group was the Matthews Brothers.

Each of the four Matthews brothers was a minister, as was their father. The Matthews had carried their gospel message in song throughout the Ozarks for several years, but in 1948 two of the brothers left the quartet in order to become full time ministers. Bob and Culley Holt were recruited to join the new group, who called themselves the Jordanaires, named after the small Jordan Creek that flows through Springfield.

The new quartet blended together in a few short months, singing mainly on radio station KWTO. The group then left for Nashville in an attempt to break onto the national recording scene. In a town already filled with aspiring musicians, the group quickly received the attention of Nashville stars and producers. Work piled up with some of the biggest names in Nashville. Red Foley, at the time the king of the Grand Ole Opry, auditioned

The Jordanaires appeared with Minnie Pearl on the Grand Ole Opry. Note: Bob Hubbard, foreground right.

them for the Opry in a studio at station WSM in Nashville. At the audition the Jordanaires were the only group in the studio and Red Foley the only person in the audience. Success soon followed, for shortly thereafter the Jordanaires became regulars on the Grand Ole Opry, singing their gospel songs. Soon their popularity reached such a height that they were recording on three different major labels, Decca, Capitol, and RCA Victor, as well as providing back-up to many stars.

Indeed, at one time, the group recorded under two different names, an occurrence that resulted in the name, The Foggy River Boys. In the early fifties the Jordainaires were approached by a Decca Record producer who wanted them to record a brand new song he was sure would become a great hit. The Jordanaires hesitated. While they agreed the song would become a hit, the Jordanaires were a gospel group. Recording a secular song, they reasoned, would tarnish their image. The group found a solution for the dilemma: the Jordanaires would record the song, but under another name. In Nashville, the Cumberland River that flows through the city is called the Foggy River. Thus, the name Foggy River Boys, used for the first time, was to record the popular "Rag Mop." The Foggy River Boys continued to record more songs, but could never make a personal appearance. They did not want anyone to know they were also the Jordanaires.

When the members of the Jordanaires left Nashville, following Red Foley to Springfield to be on the Ozark Jubilee, they were returning home. Before leaving Nashville, the quartet sold the name Jordanaires to a Nashville group which went on to became the most recorded group in history, backing up the likes of Hank Snow, Patsy Cline, Red Foley, and the King himself, Elvis, with whom they appeared on the Ed Sullivan Show in addition to several other shows and movies. By a quirk of fate, they narrowly missed being on Ricky Nelson's last airplane flight. The Jordanaires continue today with personal appearances, still singing the gospel music that highlighted their career.

Back in Springfield, the group took the name the Foggy River Boys and performed on the Ozark Jubilee until its close in 1956.

The Foggy River Boys disbanded shortly after ABC discontinued the Ozark Jubilee. Bob then served in the military during the Korean War, but upon his return was anxious to continue his singing career. Ever a member of a quartet, Bob sang with another quartet in Joplin until 1970, when several friends asked him to form still another group that would again carry the name, the Foggy River Boys. It was the beginning of a quartet and band that stayed together for over twenty years. Organizers of the group included Bob Hubbard as lead, and Dale Sullens, a music teacher, as tenor. John Shepherd, one of Dale's former high school students sang baritone, with Denzel Koontz, a postmaster, as bass. Bob Moskop, another music teacher played the piano. Each was a part owner of the show with a specific non-stage duty to fulfill. Over the years other musicians were added to the band; musicians who both played instruments and sang solos. Great musical talent marked the Foggy River Boys.

The Foggys performed for a brief two year stay in Kimberling City before moving thirty miles to Branson.

Before opening in Branson, the new group performed for two years in a small auditorium in Kimberling City, a town just a few miles south of Herman Mead's Cave, where the Presleys had performed a few years earlier. All the members of the group kept their day jobs, except Bob. All had doubts about whether Branson could support a fourth show on the emerging strip. But, much of the apprehension was dispelled when the Baldknobbers invited the group over to their theater to participate in a show, which gave much needed exposure to the Foggys at a time when they needed it. Success was assured almost immediately when at show time the building started filling with patrons.

In keeping with the other shows in Branson, the Foggys continued as a family oriented show, but also brought a new dimension to the Branson shows. The music of a quartet, singing harmony, requires a different kind of discipline than does country music. Bob contacted Monty Matthews, a member of the original Jordanaires who was still living in Springfield, to arrange music for the group. Bob, as lead, would sing the melody, with the tenor a third above the lead, the bass below, and the baritone midway between the two. But, except for the lead, if one were to hear a member of a quartet practice alone, the tune would normally be unintelligible. It is the sum of the whole, not the individual parts, that makes the harmony of a quartet so beautiful and so difficult to perform. Members of the Foggy River Boys had to practice, both alone and together, to perfect their music. In singing harmony an impromptu flair or interpretation of the music is not allowed. Performers cannot add or subtract a note or word from the song. Such actions would counteract with the rest of the quartet and void the music of the group. Harmony requires the absolute mastery of each song by every member of a quartet, and the members of the Foggys produced beautiful music because they were excellent musicians, fully mastering the intricacies of harmonizing.

The same discipline necessary for harmonizing spilled over into the rest of the Foggys show. Members of the quartet always entered the stage together, their movements well coordinated, and all stood at attention facing another performer when that musician was in the spotlight.

They also dressed alike. "We wanted to be fashionably dressed like we felt people in the audience would be pleased to dress," Bob once said. They discovered what other shows before and since have learned, that wardrobing a show is never easy. The Foggys were a troupe of singers and musicians who over the years numbered from ten to twelve individuals with different heights, weights, and physiques. It was no easy task to find identical slacks, jackets, and shirts for the troupe members. The color of two jackets could vary if made from different bolts of similar material, buttons could be mismatched, and even design differences might occur between small and larger jackets, even if the garments were labeled "identical." But they were fortunate in finding a meticulous haberdasher in Joplin, Missouri, who looked after their exacting requirements. When the Foggys appeared onstage in their striking outfits, they sparkled.

The Foggys brought a new dimension of comedy to their show, for, in contrast to the other shows in town, they did not cast a wacky hillbilly character to lighten the show. Rather, comedy was provided by the humorous banter between Bob Hubbard and the piano player, Bob Moskop. Bob Moskop, who wore a perpetual smile, would utter a loud yelp at the most inappropriate times during a show, and Hubbard would rush to him and ask what was wrong. The piano player was certain to have a topical joke or traumatic personal problem, sometimes about his thinning hair, that was sure to make the audience laugh.

In the end, though, it was their music that distinguished the Foggys. Early on, the group agreed to expand their repertoire from gospel songs to include popular tunes. Thus, in contrast to the other three

The Foggys were always stylishly dressed. Their comedy sparkled throughout each performance.

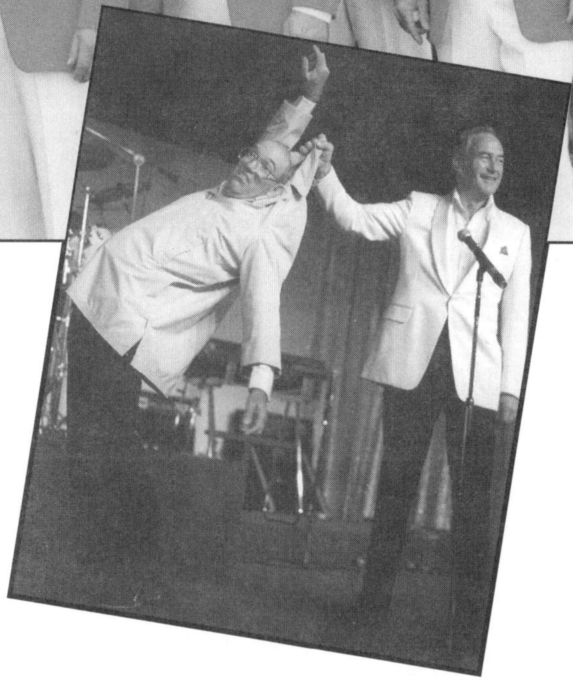

performing groups in Branson, many of their songs were not country. They would sing the songs that stirred the enthusiasm of their audiences. Thus, in addition to "Rag Mop," such songs as "New York, New York," the playful "Elvira," and gospel favorites all became popular for the Foggy River Boys. Following in the footsteps of the Plummers, there were no "stars" with the Foggys, although Bob Hubbard was their leader. For them it was the music that stood out, that was important, and that drove the interest of the group. Other quartets of the time, The Mills Brothers and the Platters, had a distinctive sound. Their music was easily recognized on the radio or a record. And so the Foggys, too, worked hard to create and maintain their own, mellow, unique sound. Any member of the quartet could and did step out and sing a solo, as did band members. But they were not stars nor were they billed as such. Not even Bob was the star. Their distinctive music symbolized the Foggys.

The show was a crowd pleaser and the Foggys delivered it well. Not only were they superb musicians, but even above that, they were entertainers. All were able to quit their day jobs soon after arriving in Branson.

Like the other shows in Branson, the Foggys lengthened their season by booking out of town dates with their summertime crowds. They kept a large pad on an easel beside the stage at the front of the theater so guests could see their wintertime

The Foggy River Boys theater was a fixture on the strip for 20 years. In 1993 it gave way to a large hotel.

travel schedule. Audience members were encouraged to book additional dates if they wanted the Foggys in their hometown, too, for an evening of fun and perhaps a fund-raiser for a town charity. By the time the Foggys ended their stay in Branson, they were performing 150 shows yearly in their own theater and over 50 road shows across mid-America, from Minnesota and Illinois to Louisiana and Texas.

The group continued in Branson until 1993 when, after 20 years of being one of Branson's favorites, the Boys decided to call it quits and sell their theater. The theater sold, strangely, to the haberdasher from Joplin who so meticulously fit their wardrobe so many years before. The theater of the Foggy River Boys, which they shared with the legendary Sons of the Pioneers during their final year, was quickly demolished and a large hotel now stands on the site.

The Foggy River Boys were the last Branson entertainment pioneers.

Change is a constant in show business. One show ends, another begins. So it goes on Broadway in New York City, in the theater district of London, and along the strip in Branson. Some shows have long runs, others, often for inexplicable reasons, have short runs. One certainty, though, is that success for any show follows only hard work. These four shows started down an uncharted course in what was not much more than a little fishing village in the Ozarks. Their success paved the way for other groups to open shows and perform in Branson, to cast their nets out, hoping for success. In time, Branson became known as the live music show capital of the world.

All Branson musical shows following these first four owe a huge debt to these pioneers.

(As a person who has seen innumerable Branson shows over the past fifty years, I have often wondered how a performer can stand on stage and sing the same song, night after night, season after season, in sickness and in health, and still retain a crisp freshness to the presentation, as if that one song, that particular night, were the most important thing in the world. Why not just get bored repeating the same performance over and over again? But, in conducting these interviews I became convinced that there is an intangible quality to show business that for the performer transcends the music, the song, and the comedy. In these interviews it became apparent that one of the driving forces for the performers is the desire to interact with the audience, to look out into the audience and see people respond to the performance. From onstage, performers can gauge the mood of the audience and feed off that response. While show business is a financial business, and, at times a very, very, brutal financial business, its overriding goal is one of entertainment, of moving people to laughter and tears, of evoking patriotic and spiritual sentiments, and of sharing the talent of the entertainer with an audience. Most of the entertainers that I interviewed evoked what seemed to me an innate desire, a passion, not unlike an addiction, to interact with an audience and entertain. They were people who could not be satisfied with any other occupation. Their path was not an easy one. They were true pioneers.)

One American President, George Bush, visited Branson in 1992 stumping for votes during his second presidential campaign.

Legacy of Branson Pioneers

Michel Feldman, on his Saturday morning program on National Public Radio, recently declared Branson to be "a little fishing village that just got out of hand." Maybe he's right. Maybe it did get out of hand. But if so, it's because of the men and women in this story who created the backbone of Branson's entertainment industry. Their efforts, both individually and collectively, turned the small, staid Ozark town into one that today hosts roughly eight million people a year. Such accomplishments are rare.

Yet, in many respects, these entertainment pioneers were just ordinary people. They had hopes, dreams, and disappointments just like the rest of us. They had spouses and children, coached little league teams, served on town councils, and chamber of commerce committees. They had loved ones die even as they worked to build their establishments. Their lives were filled with pursuing their dreams. But, perhaps, above all, they were people with visions, aspirations, and a tenacity that held them to their visions. Together, they succeeded.

The town was built on the themes that have forever been the cornerstone of country music, God, patriotism, and family. Or, as Professor Sarah Kinefelter, who lectures frequently at the Branson Show Biz Elderhostel programs puts it, the three "F's," Family, Faith, and Flag. Tony Orlando once echoed the same belief to me. They are the same elements, Tony said, that form the foundation of Country music. But in Branson, the themes extended beyond music. They also became the cornerstone of the first two venues, a reconstructed 1880's Ozark village where, even though a lot of boisterous hootin' and hollerin' and concocted banter took place, in the end everyone could stand on main street at evening's end and say the pledge of allegiance to the American flag or join with a gospel group singing Amazing Grace at Echo Hollow. Or, if visitors preferred, they could attend an outdoor drama written by a moralistic minister about transgression, guilt, redemption, forgiveness, and love. Branson's values, God, patriotism, and family, are themes that touch the souls of all men, everywhere. For regular visitors, a Branson vacation did more than offer a few days of relaxation. It confirmed the creeds that guided their lives and shaped their everyday activities.

But, these entertainment pioneers were not just men and women with insight into how to entertain an audience. They also gained the acumen to run a business, and in the case of the Herschends, a huge corporation. It became readily apparent to all that operating an entertainment business—whether it was keeping a music band together, motivating service workers at a restaurant, or selling enough tickets to a show to make the monthly bank payments—was no easy task. It certainly could not be done with a labor season that extended only from the April through October fishing season on Table Rock Lake. A thriving business needed to keep its doors open year-round. The theaters found a way to lengthen their season by purchasing those vans and buses and making the late fall, winter, and early spring trips to play out-of-town dates. Mark Trimble and the Herschends had the foresight to join forces by creating the Ozark Marketing Council, which in time turned into a strong arm of the Branson Chamber of Commerce.

Absolutely nothing succeeded like the early insight of Peter Herschend and other savvy businessmen to understand the mass marketing power of television. It began with Peter taking craftsmen to exhibit their skills on live television shows, a first for the times. The Ozark Marketing Council expanded the concept by placing ads in major midwest television markets. Later, the Branson Chamber of Commerce developed the sophisticated skills of analyzing consumer trends and contracted for strategically placed print ads in major newspapers and commercials on an ever expanding list of television stations. The episodes of the Beverly Hillbillies featuring Silver Dollar City were a boon, not only to the Herschend's business, but to the whole area. It would be difficult to overestimate the impact of television on the development of the town.

The combination of excellent family entertainment and mass marketing created the Branson entertainment industry.

The pioneering era of Branson entertainment lasted fifteen years, beginning in 1960 when Shepherd of the Hills and Silver Dollar City first opened their gates to visitors, and the Baldknobbers presented their first show. The era continued until 1974 when the Foggy River Boys moved from Kimberling City to Branson. The period established the foundation of the entertainment business and set the tone for the years to come. These were Branson's entertainment pioneering years.

Just as the pioneering years built the foundation under Branson's entertainment, the following seventeen years, from 1975 through 1991, built a supporting structure that continues to serve the entertainment industry even today. Already, as we've seen, the Shepherd of the Hills and especially Silver Dollar City were the towering forces in Branson's entertainment. The addition of the shows along Highway 76, or the "strip" highlighted these seventeen years.

The entertainment venues by themselves, while the symbols of growth, were insufficient to meet the needs of increasing numbers of vacationers arriving in the area. Tourists to Branson were in search of a vacation, not just a few hours of entertainment. They needed food, lodging, and shopping facilities along with their vacations. To invite visitors to Branson, hopefully as repeat visitors, Branson, through the Branson Chamber of Commerce, developed an aggressive advertising program. By the early 1990's Branson was on target to become a regional entertainment center with visitors pouring in, not only from Missouri, but from surrounding states and across the nation.

But, the excitement in Branson centered one-by-one on the new theaters as they were built. At least a dozen new venues were constructed during the period. The first new theater of the time period was constructed by an already familiar veteran of Branson, Bob Mabe, the originator of the Baldknobbers. In a move that surprised all of Branson, Bob broke with his brothers in 1977 and built a new theater further west on the strip, at the corner of 76 Highway and Gretna road. Although Bob was a powerful force at the Baldknobbers, the old show didn't miss a beat when he left. And, his new production was an immediate success. He named both the building and show after his own stage name, Bob-O-Link, with the theater becoming the Bob-O-Link's Theater and the show Bob-O-Link's Country Hoedown. The new show followed in the tradition of the Baldknobbers, a fast

Bob Mabe opened the Bob O Link's theatre in 1977.

Chisai Childs from Grapevine, TX, was a performer and producer. Her greatest find, Shoji Tabuchi, who ascended to stardom in Branson.

paced country music show with Bob as emcee, and a country music format featuring the jig-dancing of the Burdette Family dancers. Bob continued to supplement the show with Nashville stars who appeared as regular guests.

Four new theaters with four new tenants were completed in 1981, while the Presley family expanded their theater to 2,000 seats, making it the largest theater in Branson. The new shows followed the format of the already existing shows, country music variety shows.

The Wilkerson brothers, from a little town on the east side of Missouri, Bonne Terre, opened the Wilkinson Brothers Country Music Show, and played contemporary country and gospel music. On the recently abandoned Branson airport, the performers of the nationally televised Hee Haw show were installed in the Hee Haw theater. And, the Ozark Country Jubilee, borrowing heavily on the name of the Ozarks Jubilee TV show in Springfield, opened across from the Bob-O-Links theater. For the first few years, this show was headlined by emcee David Struble, a practicing dentist from nearby Ozark, Missouri.

Finally, further down the strip, Chisai Childs purchased the recently completed Starlite Theater. Chisai, a producer from Texas, brought a hitherto unknown flair and flamboyancy to Branson. As a producer Chisai displayed an uncanny eye for talent, and some of the performers she introduced still perform in Branson. Her most notable recruit, Shoji Tabuchi, quickly spiraled to the top as one of Branson's superstars. During show time, Chisai, who emceed her own shows, brought eye-popping attention to herself with the extravagant gowns she wore to dazzle audiences. Chisai left the stage after announcing each number, then reemerged at its conclusion, clad in another of her gorgeous gowns. She would change gowns up to 20 times in each performance. In response to Chisai, several other shows at the time felt compelled to add to, or spruce up their own productions.

But, these four shows were just the beginning of the proliferation. In 1983 the Lowe's Country Music Show, headlined by the Lowe family—consisting of mom and dad, Ken and Levon, and their four attractive and talented daughters, Teresa, Sheila, Sandy, and Kathy, soared to popularity. Originally from Bowling Green, Kentucky, the Lowe's actually began performing in nearby Stone County. When their theater located on Indian Point burned, they moved to Branson. Harold Morrison, a former member of Ozark Jubilee who then became a popular Nashville star, joined the group in the 1980's. The Lowe's were the first Branson group to appear on the Grand Ole Opry in Nashville.

In 1983 another musical family, The Lowes, opened the Lowes Country Music Theatre. For a while, some of the Grand Ole Opry stars like Loretta Lynn, Conway Twitty, Johnny Russell and others became regular performers.

In 1983, Roy Clark became the first national performer to lend his name to a marquee when he joined local entrepreneur and promoter Jim Thomas

Roy Clark was the first national star to lend his name to a theater in Branson.

at Jim's new theater as part of a lodging/convention/entertainment complex, the Lodge of the Ozarks. Roy, a superb guitar player from the cast of Hee-Haw, was also instrumental in bringing national stars to Branson for guest appearances. A plaque listing the guest stars of the theater still adorns a wall of the theater lobby.

Still, more musical venues were built. In 1984, the Branson Opry House was built with Buddy Green as the headliner. The Herschends cleared off a hillside at the edge of Silver Dollar City and constructed a huge outdoor arena, naming it Echo Hollow. Among the first performers at Echo Hollow were the nationally famous bluegrass band, the Dillards. Known to their fans as the Darling Family, they had starred in the popular Andy Griffith TV show. The following year, in 1985, the King's Mansion was built on Gretna Road, by a cousin to the King himself, who performed a nightly tribute to Elvis Presley. That same year, the Braschler Music Show opened with Cliff Braschler and his family following the successful format already established by other shows in town, a country variety show with both a comedy and a gospel segment. In 1987, Box Car Willie, undoubtedly America's richest hobo,

Silver Dollar City became involved with nighttime music shows in 1984 with the opening of Echo Hollow.

opened his theater and nightly filled it to capacity by advertising openly out of Nashville. Before Boxcar's career ended, he owned a theater, a railroad museum, and two motels in Branson.

By the mid-eighties, the line-up of performers in Branson was already in transition. Proving the adage that show business is always changing, some shows had already completed their "run," and others were ready to take their place. New performers and new acts were anxious for their turn in the spotlight. Ownership of the old Hee-Haw theater passed to novelist Janet Dailey and her husband Bill, who, after three years, sold the theater to Mickey Gilley, one of the stars of the movie "Urban Cowboy." The Daileys were responsible for bringing a talented quartet into the area known as the Tennessee Valley Boys, which they renamed the Branson Brothers. The energetic Brothers quickly amassed a huge following of fans and eventually signed a national recording contract. They seemed destined for stardom. But, in the end, the quartet fell short of such renown, another example of the fickle nature of stardom. During this period Yakoff Smirnoff and Jim Stafford, both former TV personalities, established themselves in Branson.

Meanwhile, theater owners and managers discovered theater seats could be utilized for more than just a once a day two-hour evening performance. Motivated by the need to increase revenue, pay mortgages, and realize profits, they added morning shows and afternoon matinees as well as the evening performances, sometimes having as many as four different shows in a single day by four different performing groups. Many lengthened their Branson season well beyond the fishing season on Table Rock Lake, starting shows early in the springtime and extending them late into the fall. To extend the season even further, Christmas

Tourist season to Branson was lengthened by events like the springtime international music festival that drew crowds earlier in the season.

shows were begun, with theaters decorating their venues with twinkling lights and holly and altering their regular performance during the Yule time to include a Christmas music segment. Branson flourished and grew.

The sprawl down Highway 76 reflected the construction of the theaters. To cater to tourist needs, hotels and restaurants sprouted up where before small farms, goat pastures, and strawberry patches had once existed. Traffic jams were becoming common on the two-lane highway. Comedians joked about Branson being a town of parking lots, separated only by a few motels and smorgasbord restaurants. Even a retired major league baseball pitcher, Jack Hamilton, teamed up with country music singer Tommy Overstreet to operate a popular buffet south of town. Employment needs were extending beyond what local residents could supply, and college students and senior citizens from outside the area began filling summer employment vacancies, working as ticket takers, ushers, waitresses, and even as energetic saloon dancers at Silver Dollar City.

By 1990 Ray Stevens had built a new theater at the intersection of 76 Highway and the new Shepherd of the Hills Expressway at the base of Dewey Bald Mountain. The Osmond Brothers were firmly entrenched in the old Bob-O-Links theater and Shoji Tabuchi flourished in his new theater, replete with magnificent bathrooms, out on the new road north of town, the Shepherd of the Hills Expressway.

In 1991 crooner Andy Williams announced he would build the Moon River theater in Branson, even as the Herschends publicized the building of the largest theater ever, the 4000 seat Grand Palace, on a commanding site midway down the strip.

Branson residents stood in awe of their own little town. Branson was growing into something unlike any other town ever, its renown increasing throughout Missouri and the midwest. Amazingly, in 1990, the U. S. census recorded a population for

In 1991, the construction of two new theaters was announced; The Moon River Theater of Andy Williams and the 4000 seat Grand Palace (above) by the Herschends.

Branson of only 2,976 residents. No wonder the town was crowded when 3,000,000 visitors showed up to be entertained each year!

Even in 1991, a recession year for the U.S, visitor levels to Branson increased, bucking a national trend. How could any town prosper more? And yet, in 1991, Branson was to receive its biggest boost yet. As the old cliché goes, "you ain't seen nothin' yet."

In 1991, only three major television networks existed. One of the most watched and respected programs on television was the CBS news program, "60 Minutes." Watched by millions of devoted followers, the program carried an inordinate impact across the nation. In the summer of 1991 one of the show's hard-hitting correspondents, Morley Safer, with production crew in hand, arrived in Branson. His intent, as stated on the show, was to film what he would call a cultural, financial, and entertainment phenomenon. But, at

Branson's venues transformed themselves with the addition of the Christmas season. Branson now had an almost year-round tourist season.

his arrival, it was unknown what Safer would report about the town. Known for its penetrating news stories, "60 Minutes" would either find value in the enthusiastic crowds that descended on Branson to be entertained by family-valued entertainment, or it would find the entertainment mecca a garish and shallow veneer-coated exhibition. There could be no middle ground: "60 Minutes" would either extol or castigate.

When the show aired in December, 1991, Branson residents listened in excitement for, during the fifteen minute broadcast, Morley Safer could hardly contain his enthusiasm. With euphoric fervor, he delivered a spellbinding description of the little town, concentrating on the bevy of country music stars performing in Branson. He filmed a traffic cop whirling and rotating as he directed a barrage of traffic on a busy Highway 76 intersection, untangling traffic jams on the tiny, winding two-lane strip. He noted that Branson hosted 4,000,000 people annually. (This figure may have been an inflated estimate. Probably closer to 3,000,000 would have been more acurate.) He showed Loretta Lynn gustily belting a refrain of her signature song, "I'm Proud to be a Coal Miner's Daughter," and guitar picker Roy Clark strumming himself into a frenzy before explaining that tourists spent $1.5 billion annually on the strip. Next, he filmed a tourist family praying at mealtime in a local restaurant, scanned the audience at Presleys' Country Jubilee as they belly-laughed to the antics of Herkimer, and highlighted the work of Steve on the drums. He presented a smiling country music star, Mel Tillis, who explained that even he could own a theater. Mel refused to deny that he could make six million dollars a year while sleeping in his own bed every night in Branson. Then, he explained that to do so he had to sign autographs before and after every show to make that kind of money. The TV segment then highlighted the charismatic Shoji

Tabuchi joking with his audience, then ending his evening show with a gigantic patriotic climax. Safer extolled the phenomenon of Branson.

That one segment of the "60 Minutes" television show, and its reruns, were responsible for attracting nearly an additional one million visitors to Branson the following year. In 1992, almost 4 million visitors poured into Branson. Traffic jams, long waiting lines at restaurants, and a dearth of motel rooms awaited visitors. Nationally, it was as if, after thirty years of existence, Branson's entertainment scene had become an overnight success.

Finally, after 30 years, two towering entertainment industries, the Branson music shows, and Silver Dollar City, each complimenting the other with family entertainment, existed side by side. The "60 Minutes" show elevated Branson as an entertainment center for the midwest, on par with The Wisconsin Dells in Wisconsin and Myrtle Beach in North Carolina. Some even began viewing the area as a vacation destination in the same category with Las Vegas and Orlando, Florida.

Every theater in town, including Andy Williams' newly opened Moon River Theater and the Grand Palace were regally rewarded by the surge of visitors.

Due to the exposure on "60 Minutes," some of the largest magazines and newspapers across the nation picked up the story and a barrage of visiting reporters and stars from all entertainment fields, including Hollywood, came to see what all the commotion was about. Even Bob Hope showed up to find out what was going on. Branson residents buzzed with all the excitement.

The TV show triggered the doubling of theaters in Branson, with the construction of new venues including Dolly Parton's Dixie Stampede, the Welk Resort, the Showboat Branson Belle, which was built on the shores of Table Rock Lake, then launched sliding down a shoreline greased with tons of bananas, a huge new Mel Tillis Theater north of town, Tony Orlando's Yellow Ribbon Theater, the Mansion and Remington Theaters, the Charley Pride Theater on a hilltop overlooking Gretna Road, and Bobby Vinton's Blue Velvet Theater. Even in those recession times, the boom continued for four years.

The pinnacle of the era came in 1994 with the announcement that a troupe of Rockettes, licensed by the producers of the New York City Music Hall, would perform during the Christmas season at the Grand Palace for a five year stint, to the same demanding standards as the parent group.

Branson was filled with the sentiments of the season. Where else, in all of America, could one dazzle themselves in a town where every venue was decorated with Christmas lights, enjoy the high-stepping beauties of the Rockettes, hear the wonderful Lennon sisters with full orchestra accompaniment, watch Tony Orlando seize a stage along with his Christmas Santa Claus, or see the Andy Williams Christmas Special every night of the Christmas season. Not to be outdone, Shoji

A Branson boom erupted after a broadcast of CBS's "60 Minutes" segment on Branson by Morley Safer.

After "60 Minutes," Branson residents contended with an avalanche of an additional one million visitors; and countless motorcoaches and immense construction machinery.

Tabuchi's Christmas extravaganza attracted enough audience members to fill his theater three times a day and Silver Dollar City sparkled with one million twinkling lights, seemingly decorating every board and tree limb in the park. Every venue in town produced a Christmas show. Christmas visitors arrived and Branson entertained them lavishly. It was a magical period and Christmas became the highlight of the Branson entertainment year.

(Young dancers from around the nation arrived in Branson to audition for the Rockettes. Many of the successful aspirants hailed from New York City and had never lived in a mid-western town where car transportation was a necessity. Several had never even driven an automobile. Yet, written into their contracts at the Grand Palace was a clause requiring that each dancer be provided with a automobile. To the accounting staff at the Grand Palace, the Rockettes quickly earned the name, the Wreckettes.)

In reality, boom periods do not last forever. By the mid-nineties at the opening of the spring season, first one restaurant around town and then another failed to open. Small "For Sale" signs could be seen taped to the windows of a few motels, and finally, theaters began staying dark throughout the performing season. Even as visitor numbers increased, it became apparent that something was wrong.

The appetites of entertainment producers were bigger than their ability to attract an audience. There simply were not enough visitors to fill all the seats, nor could sufficient numbers be attracted—especially when theaters offered two, three, sometimes even four different performances a day. In this case, bigger was not better. More theater seats did not translate into greater revenue. Within a matter of years, two of the larger venues, The Remington and the Mel Tillis Theaters, became churches and the Welk Resort theater underutilized. The Yellow Ribbon Theater closed, as did the Grand Palace. To this day, it sits forlorn on its commanding site, awaiting a rejuvenation of spirit. Obviously, Branson's entertainment venues were overbuilt.

In spite of this, Branson still flourishes today as an entertainment center. From its humble beginnings Branson's entertainment has grown until, in 2009, the town counted 50 different theaters with more than 100 shows and 64,000 theater seats. The area contains more than 22,000 lodging rooms and 37,000 restaurant seats. The entertainment sector attracted more than 7.8 million visitors with expenditures of over $3.8 billion dollars. Visitor estimates now range close to 8,000,000 per year, with tourists arriving from all 50 states and many foreign countries. The town's advertising gurus look upon the town as a regional center and direct most of their marketing dollars into Missouri and surrounding states.

Today, fifty years after the start of the first entertainment, the legacy of those early entertainment pioneers remains. Branson is still a town dedicated to delivering family oriented entertainment. A family can attend a show together, from the smallest child to the oldest grandparent, and each becomes captivated by the same entertainment. Family entertainment is the constant that runs through all of Branson.

Still thriving are productions that present the old, the safe, and the familiar numbers that tug at the heart strings of the audience. There are those visitors who, as Morley Safer noted, want to be surprised only by the familiar.

It would be impossible over the years to count the number of times a show has ended with a resounding patriotic number. It's almost a formula. After a brisk-paced evening of music, the number calls for the star vocalist to sing a country favorite, something like the old Lee Greenwood song, "I'm Proud to be an American." Soon the vocalist is quietly joined by an ensemble of back-up singers who increase the volume of the song. Blended with these singers, in turn, are the voices of the band members. Almost without the audience noticing, the star of the show has been joined by a host of on-stage singers, raising the song to a crescendo. And, as they sing, the intensity of the stage lights increases and begins to weave a red, white, and blue pattern across the stage. An overhead projector illuminates the American flag on a screen at the rear of the stage. No wonder, so often, audience members spontaneously rise from their seats and applaud the closing number, well before its conclusion. Some of their deepest emotions are stirred. Sure, it's show business arranged by talented professional producers intent on stirring such a reaction from a listening audience. But it also reaches beyond the emotional impact. These audience members leave the show sustained in what they believe.

The latest major theater built in Branson is the sixty-five million dollar, 2000 seat Sight and Sound Theater constructed on a beautiful hillside site on the north side of Branson. A gigantic 300 foot stage, (literally the size of a football field) envelops the audience as it wraps around three sides of the auditorium. Productions are enhanced by the latest light and sound technology. Magnificent presentations portray poignant biblical stories. This year "Noah—the Musical" and "The Miracle of Christmas" will be presented. Other epic productions are rotated into the theater. The presentations, a combination of religion and entertainment, exist "to honor God and encourage faith."

Overt patriotism and religion presented through entertainment is a commonly held image of Branson. Yet, to believe this would be an incomplete understanding. The phenomenon of Branson built by the businesses and reinforced by Morley Safer nearly twenty years ago has both grown and changed—and attracts more than twice the number of visitors than it did when Safer reported on the town.

Silver Dollar City is still an 1880's craft village with working craftsmen, but now also

The lovely Rockettes performed at the Grand Palace during the late 1990's.

includes a series of festivals spread throughout the year with both international and American music and entertainment, including musicians performing Bluegrass, gospel, and folk music. To meet the expectations of a new generation, dozens of themed rides have been added. One by one thrill rides, complete with the biggest and scariest roller coasters constructed to scare the smithereens out of screaming teenagers whose ear-splitting shouts call for more, now dot the premises. The contraptions soar above treetops and race around curves. They've been given names like Wildfire, PowderKeg, Fire-In-the-Hole, Thunderation, and The Giant Swing. No wonder kids love 'em and return time after time. (I wish they had been there when I was a kid.)

One reason for Silver Dollar City's success is because of its efforts to reach successfully multiple generations of visitors. Today the arts and crafts, international, and music festivals in the spring and fall attract adults and seniors as well as families into the park, and in the summer the young people revel in KidsFest and the thrill rides. This is followed by the Christmas season, perhaps the most successful time of the year as the City ends with a nationally recognized Christmas celebration. All is available in a clean and safe environment. Over the years the park managers and staff have carefully and skillfully crafted an entertainment venue that has brought joy, happiness, and wonder to multiple generations. It is no wonder that from the beginning attendance at the park has steadily increased.

It is infinitely more difficult to define the music industry that is spread along the Branson strip.

Not all of the entertainment in Branson exhibits the drama of a patriotic ending to a music show or the epic production of a Biblical story. In fact, most of the venues present a much calmer demeanor. Who, for example, could be more family-friendly than Andy Williams? Yet Andy, whose singing style is as comfortable to the ear as a pair of favorite old worn house slippers to the feet, still makes twice a year appearances for several weeks–long spring and fall engagements. Shoji Tabuchi performs his daily exatravaganza. The Platters, the Duttons, Yakov Smirnoff and Jim

Stafford meet daily schedules as do dozens of other groups. In the summertime Peter Pan, in the form of Olympic star Cathy Rigby, flies across the stage at the Mansion Theater. Tony Orlando returns each fall to seize a stage, honor veterans, and celebrate Christmas. The wonderful music of the Lennon Sisters is still heard at Christmastime. This year's favorite new show is "Chun Yi-The Legend of Kung Fu," a heart-stopping combination of "traditional martial arts skills, aerial ballet, dance and music," in one of the largest productions of the season. A common denominator of the Branson shows is the excellence of entertaiment.

Excellence by itself does not assure a show of success, but without excellence, no show succeeds.

One thing, though, absent from shows in Branson is the biting social and political satire and hard rock concerts featured at other destinations. Bare bosoms do not appear in Branson shows, nor have gambling casinos gained a foothold.

One of the paramount features of Branson is the effort of Branson to honor service veterans and honor the heroic actions of the courageous military veterans granted purple hearts, distinguished medals, and the Medal of Honor. Most shows recognize veterans nightly and a designated Veterans Week is set aside in the fall with special activities to honor veterans.

Perhaps the most significant of all veterans reunions took place at the Welk resort fifty or so years after the last sortie flown over Europe in WW II. World War II was a segregated period and during the war a renowned group of black fighter pilots, known as the Tuskegee airmen, flew cover for white bomber pilots in the artillery saturated skies of Europe. During the war the two units had been stationed at different airfields, meeting only in the sky as they flew their combat missions. At the reunion at the Welk resort the surviving warriors from this epic period met face to face, many for the first time, to shake hands, hug, and share tears. The bravery of the individuals and the tenor of the entertainment meshed in Branson.

The phenomenon that draws millions to Branson is constantly changing and evolving with each year, each period of social change, and each generation. Some note it as a slow, evolving process as old shows close and others arrive to take their places. Others describe a more predictable change, an incremental change, mirroring the social habits of the time. Others even use an academic term, disjointed instrumentalism, (wow) to define a rather haphazard non-predictable change that, none-the-less is guided by the people in the entertainment field.

While Branson does not have something for everyone, it has much to offer to many. Yet, can anyone fully describe the shows on Broadway, in London, or even in Las Vegas? I doubt it. Yet, each destination has found an entertainment niche. The entertainment out of Branson emanates from the heartland of America. Its formula for success has changed little since the early entertainment pioneers began their efforts with excellent productions of family-oriented entertainment. It has created the most unusual town in America.

And so, where are these pioneers today?

Mark Trimble still makes the daily sojourn to his Branson office, looking after his large collection of classic automobiles and airplanes, and overseeing a staff that by now are more friends than employees. And, on some evenings, at dusk, Branson visitors can look upward and spot an airplane flying low over the Branson strip. That's Mark, who finds old habits hard to break. He's up there flying around in one of his twenty-four vintage airplanes, still checking on the number of visitors in the parking lots of the various shows.

The Herschends developed Silver Dollar City into the largest family owned entertainment corporation in America. Headquarters for their corporate offices are now in Atlanta, Georgia, and

Silver Dollar City celebrated 50 years of entertainment in May, 2010. Pictured above are Sherry and Jack Herschend and Peter and JoDee Herschend.

recently, the company CEO, Joel Manby, was featured on the CBS show, "Undercover Boss." Herschend Family Entertainment encompasses 25 major venues in nine states, stretching across the country from New Jersey and Myrtle Beach, to South Carolina and San Francisco. Several properties in between are clustered in both Branson and Georgia. Those properties include several attractions that bear Dolly Parton's name, including Dolly Parton's Dixie Stampede and Dollywood in Tennessee, two aquariums, and several Ride the Ducks attractions. Success has come to the Herschends even as they have fulfilled Hugo's vision of providing family-oriented entertainment.

Jack and Peter Herschend, who are largely responsible for building the corporation, are retired from corporate work, although both, along with their wives, are active in multiple charitable organizations and foundations in the Branson area and throughout the nation. Peter is a bicyclist and has raised over one million dollars from bike rides supporting multiple sclerosis. Jack is following in his mother's tradition of environmentalism and beautification. He personally oversees a tree plantation where he hopes to grow one million trees to be given away and replanted in the Ozarks. Mary Herschend passed away in 1983.

The Baldknobber show continues its nightly performances in Branson, proudly proclaiming itself the longest-running continuous show in Branson. However, none of the founding brothers are associated with the show, although second generation Mabes now own, produce, and perform on the show. Three of the pioneer brothers, Jim, Lyle, and Bill, have passed on. Bob is still active at age eighty, having formed yet another band composed of senior citizens, this one through his church. Band members call themselves "The Kitchen Band." Bob arranges performances for the group, drives the bus to performances, emcees, and sings for the near weekly performances that the band gives. The group, which bears an uncanny resemblance to the original Baldknobber Hillbilly Band, features keyboards played by Bob's wife, Sue, a banjo played by 90 year old Millie Laurenas, along with fiddle and guitar music, and comedy. In this band, as in the original Baldknobbers band, performers play a washtub, washboard, and the omnipresent "jackassaphone."

The Presley family still performs nightly throughout the season at the Presleys' Country Jubilee theater. It remains, and flourishes as a family oriented show, both in program presentation and with generations of Presleys involved in the total production. Over the years, family members have been extremely active in local organizations, served on Branson Chamber of Commerce committees, and state and regional tourism committees.

Four generations of Presleys now appear on stage nightly. Gary, as the comedian Herkimer, continues to update his stage antics and serves as the president of the family corporation. He and wife Pat dote on six grandchildren. Steve, who cut his show-biz teeth helping Merle Meade serve refreshments and attaching and taking off the adhesive bumper stickers that advertised the show, continues as the band drummer. He is also married to the town's mayor, Raeanne. He and Raeanne have become the proud grandparents of three grandchildren. Family patriarch Lloyd Presley retired from the stage in 2007 and passed away in October, 2010. Bessie Mae preceded him in death in 2007.

When Darrell and Rosie Plummer sold their theater, the Plummer Family Country Music Theater, in 1990, they moved to the small town of Farmington on the eastern side of Missouri. After a short period of travel, Darrel and Rosie found themselves longing to return to the music career they had known. They soon reformed their country music band and still perform, although on a much reduced schedule, in road shows throughout the midwest and south. Their daughter, Melody, still performs in shows in Arkansas, Missouri, and Texas. Son Randy continues his musical career in Branson where he performs in a number of different shows. The Plummers return to Branson for an annual reunion show.

Members of the Foggy River Boys are largely retired, although some still keep part-time employment. Dale Sullens lives in Branson as does Bob Moskopf, who runs a bowling alley. John Shepherd keeps busy in Springfield. Denzel Koontz has passed away.

Bob Hubbard still lives in Branson. After his days with the Foggy River Boys, Bob turned to the ministry, pastoring several area churches. He still supplies pulpits to churches in the area. Although now infrequently, he occasionally calls the Foggy River Boys together for reunion performances. In collaboration with a partner, he is the manager of the famous cowboy performers, The Sons of the Pioneers.

Through hard work and perseverance, the entertainment pioneers of Branson set the framework for a town that has brought joy and happiness to millions of visitors. Although in constant evolution, it will, for years, remain one of the most unusual towns in America.

White Oak Publishing
P.O. Box 188
Reeds Spring, MO 65737

Additional copies of this book may be ordered on-line or through the postal service. Instructions for ordering are on-line at:
www.whiteoakpublishing.net